Q60

Coaching Mastery in Sixty Questions

★★★
★★

by

Alex Verlek
Mastercoach

Published by Coaching Works International, The Netherlands

Editing: Annelies Hollewand
Fiona Wasteney

Proofreading: Aisling Gray, Coach and Communications Consultant
Christina Weber, CPCC
Helen Cottee, PCC/CPCC
Photography: Marianne Louge

Design and Illustrations: Ton Swart

Management: Annelies Hollewand

Contact information: www.alexverlek.nl
hello@alexverlek.nl

Previous publications: *Awareness Builder 101*, ISBN9789492597298 (2019)
Golden Rules for Coaching, ISBN9789083206905 (2021)

ISBN:
978-90-832069-8-1 (paperback)
978-90-835026-9-4 (eBook)

I am:

An awareness builder who inspires and
supports the Army of Positive Change

My mission:

Positively impact the lives of 10 million people
through the power of coaching and its ripple effect

Master Certified Coach / Author / Imperfectionizt

Acknowledgements & Gratitude

In all my books I express my gratitude to my wife Daphne. You are not only my much beloved life-partner, you are also my best friend, supporter and co-adventurer.

I celebrate my son, Wessel. Your path is such an inspiration to many! I'm also grateful for the special woman by your side, Emmy.

Our dogs are still such a bundle of JOY and unconditional love. Lupo (†), Bibi & Sixty. You teach me to be present in the moment and to play.

Annelies Hollewand for being such a reliable and powerful force in the background. You are so much more than a PA!

Gratitude to all the inspiring teachers, (now) colleagues and students who have kept sharpening and growing me for almost two decades!

The Co-Active Training Institute (CTI), which first trained me as a student in coaching and keeps training me by having me as a senior faculty member.

The International Coaching Federation (ICF) for holding our profession to the highest standards.

And you, dear reader; you are curious about coaching and eager to grow yourself. I hope this book inspires you and gives you the answers you're looking for.

My Longing for this Book

I've decided to write this book to mark a special moment in my life: turning 60. This comes with huge gratitude for everything I've been given all these years. Life has been very kind to me. What do you do when you have more or less everything you want? My conclusion is that the best way to celebrate the kindness of life is to 'pay it forward'.

My hope and intention is that the 7th decade of my life will be filled with inspiring and supporting others, with kindness and generosity.

Instead of presents for my 60th birthday, I asked for questions. Questions about coaching, from coaches and by others who are wondering what this profession is about.

You honoured my request and gave me the 60 questions I asked for. It was such an inspiring and enriching experience to dive into these questions. Thank you!

My longing is that the answers I've written will give you clarity. About what coaching is in general. About how you can take your own coaching to the next level. How you can take being a client in a coaching relationship to the next level.

How we can demystify coaching a little bit, collectively.

Additionally, I would love the impact of coaching to grow, making the world a better and more peaceful place.

The Author

Alex Verlek was born in The Netherlands in 1964 and left school to start working at the age of 15. While holding a full-time job, Alex went back to school at 20 to study Human Resources for five years, followed by another two years of Management Sciences. His career took several funny turns until coaching found Alex in 2007. This was also when he started making dreams come true a permanent part of life. Sometimes step by step. Sometimes just by jumping into a new adventure.

Alex wrote his first book, *Awareness Builder 101*, in 2019. In this book he reflected on 52 situations he experienced in his own life, inviting the reader to make up their own mind about them. The second book, *Golden Rules for Coaching* (2021), was written to celebrate Alex' 15 years in the profession of coaching. The 15 Golden Rules capture the key insights he collected on this journey. He has other books 'in the making', but with his 60th birthday approaching, he decided to write this book first. Indeed, celebrating life and paying it forward are his mottos for his 7th decade, so writing this book felt like the right thing to do.

Alex loves working with people and recharges his batteries in nature. This is one of the reasons Alex and his wife Daphne fell in love with a small medieval village in France, where they are in the midst of nature and surrounded by vineyards and mountains.

Index Sixty Questions* about Coaching

* The questions have been preserved as they were originally asked, with minimal editing for clarity or consistency.

* A coachee or client is the individual receiving coaching. Both terms are used in this book.

Q1: Why is it called 'coaching'?

When I saw this question, I knew right away that this had to be the first question to dive into! Gaining more clarity around this concept will help both the coach and the (potential) client.

To answer this question, let's first go to Athens where in the years 470–399 BC, a Greek philosopher lived. His name was Socrates. He believed that if people knew the right thing to do, they would do it. That no one voluntarily does wrong but that 'evil' is the result of ignorance. In order to make people more aware, Socrates did not teach. Instead, he listened. Instead of telling people what to do, he asked questions, with the intention of making them see where they missed the point, where their own flaws or weaknesses of reasoning lay. Therefore, some see Socrates as the first coach.

From there we can jump to the 15th century, to a little village near Budapest, Hungary, with the name 'Kocs'. The Hungarians developed a new, lighter, more advanced carriage intended to move someone from A to B in a fast and efficient way. The pronunciation of the name 'Kocs' is strikingly similar to 'coach' and with that we have traced the root of the word.

Let's jump forward again, this time to the 1970s. Timothy Gallwey wrote *The Inner Game of Tennis* (1972) which talks about a battle against lapses in concentration, nervousness, self-doubt, and self-condemnation. Gallwey said: "The most important skill the player needs to develop to win the Inner Game is relaxed concentration. The secret to winning any game lies in not trying too hard". In sports, the coach plays an important role, helping the athlete to create a different mindset which influences their actions in a new, transformative way. In the decades that followed, 'professional life coaching' was born, and many see Thomas Leonard (1955-2003) as the founding father of this new profession.

A lot of different ways of coaching exist, there are many different schools and approaches. Yet those who see it as a serious and professional activity, will recognise that they are indeed offering a 'Kocs' experience to the individual or the team they are working with; a 'vehicle' to move them from where they are now to where they long to be.

***

Q2: How to explain what coaching is?

If you want an 'official' answer to this question, I can quote a definition such as the one given to us by the ICF: "Coaching is partnering with our clients in a thought-provoking and creative process to maximise their personal and professional potential".

Some like definitions, others like metaphors. Borrowed from my book *Golden Rules for Coaching* (2021), here is the story of the garden as a way to explain what coaching is:

I picture the coach and the coachee going for a walk through the garden on their first meeting. Whilst getting to know each other a bit, they look around and start discussing the coachee's ideas about the garden. The coach is asking all kinds of questions to help the coachee gain clarity on how they see their future garden and why they want it to be like that.

There's a fair chance that the coachee will ask how the coach is going to help them make this happen and how they're going to do that. Maybe as a surprise for the coachee, they'll be told that all the coach will do is show them where they have their tools so they can do all the gardening themselves. 'What if I don't know how to use these tools?' the coachee might ask. 'What if I don't know which plants to plant in my garden?'.

You can probably think of a lot more 'what-if questions' you've heard your coachees ask you at the beginning of and during the sessions. As well as 'why don't you do this for me or at least tell me how to do it? I know nothing about gardening!'. So the first thing for the coach is to share their trust in the coachee and that they hold them as the expert in their own garden. Even when they find it hard to believe they actually even have 'a green finger', the coach keeps expressing belief in their potential.

'You might not be able to see the garden, yet I see the seeds in you. These seeds belong to you, they are your birthright, and nature was really very generous with how many seeds live inside you. They are rich, diverse, talented and waiting for you to start bringing their potential to life. This is not something new, you came to this world with all this magic deeply rooted in you. Bringing all this to life is something you can't delegate. What we can do though is join forces. My part is to help you to start dreaming about what wants to come to life in your garden. My job is to be wildly curious about the flowers you want to see, the vegetables and fruits you want to harvest. About how you want others to feel when they visit your garden and how it inspires them.

Your job is to become aware of what you already have and what you really want. It's your garden, not mine, remember? It belongs exclusively to you!

After you've made your choices, you'll need to act in line with what you really, really want. Otherwise, these choices will not be much more than inspiring thoughts. You'll need to get your hands dirty, work the soil, sow the seeds and plant. I'll be there to cheer you on and support you to hold on to the vision you have for your garden.

Be prepared for things to unfold differently to your expectations and despite your best intentions. Your plants may fail to thrive, and weeds could take over your garden. You may wonder why you thought gardening was a good idea and consider giving up on it. People will question your actions, try to convince you to do things differently or not at all. Also 'when the shit hits the fan' I'll be there for you! I'll listen to your frustrations and whatever other emotions you experience, they're safe and welcome. Whilst you see your garden coming to life more and more, I'll keep reminding you about the 'Big Why' for all of this and what else you want to honour with this. Sometimes you'll feel stuck in how you see things evolve. I'll take you on another tour of your garden, inviting you to look at things from a different angle. Encourage you to choose again what will support you most and brainstorm possible actions from there. Actions you will take.

Maybe I'll invite you to just sit in a little corner and observe your garden in silence. I'll sit next to you. I'll be there with you.

You will also harvest your first fruits and vegetables. You will taste the success of your hard work. You're already on the path towards your success and I will acknowledge you for how you show up.

No matter how things will go, what you may perceive as successful or as failure, I'll hold you accountable and invite you to look at the lessons to be learned from this. These lessons will lead to new insights, to new awareness. With that you'll complete one cycle: awareness leads to choices, choices to actions, actions to accountability and new awareness.

My job is to guide you through this process, your job is to be it, own it, do it.'

***

Q3: Getting to the bottom line: What is coaching?

Coaching is like taking a coachee on a scavenger hunt to explore new terrain, to discover additional resources which they can use to make conscious, resonant choices towards creating the life they want to live.

***

Q4: What is an Empowered Relationship?

Coaches often talk about how they offer an 'empowered relationship' to their coachees. Sounds very nice, but what does that actually mean?

It is so much more than offering warmth and safety where every part of the coachee's life is welcome. Where all they share will be treated with respect and confidentiality.

An Empowered Relationship also means the coach is really believing in their coachee, that they acknowledge who they are at their core and champion them for what they can become. The coach is taking a stand for the growth of the coachee, even when they are questioning it themselves.

This is a relationship without hierarchy, yet with clear responsibilities and different roles for the coach and the coachee. It's a relationship where the coach and the coachee consciously discuss how they want to be with each other, even when the going gets tough. Where heartfelt conversations happen and the coach is being fully present and focused on the growth of their coachee. No distractions, no multitasking, just deeply connected with everything the coachee is communicating, verbally and non-verbally.

An 'Empowered Relationship' is not a one-way street. It's a shared responsibility that is consciously designed, and redesigned when needed.

The image below explains how both the coach and the coachee carry the relationship. Where both empower this relationship and grant it authority.

The coach is an individual and the coachee is an individual. The relationship is a separate entity. The coach is responsible for the process of the coaching, whereas the coachee is responsible for the content. It is a container, an environment that exists for the sake of the growth of the coachee. The coaching, as such, is an experience that's co-created by the coach and the coachee, and it can only truly come to life when they both show up fully.

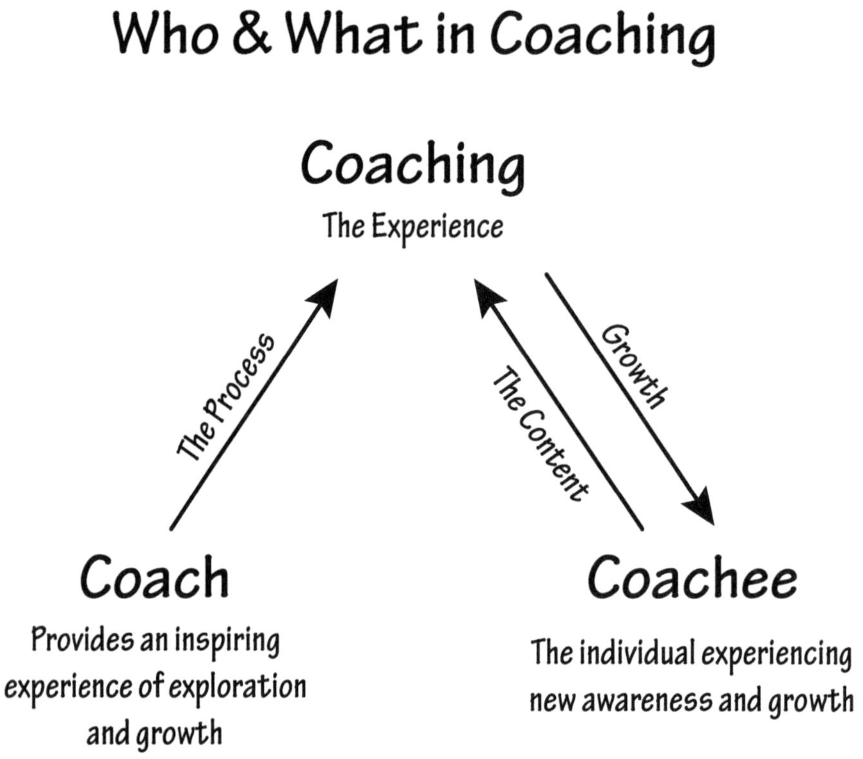

To be in such an Empowered Relationship, both need to come from a place of authenticity and acknowledge their role. These roles don't know a hierarchy, yet they are different, each with its own characteristics and responsibilities. Equal yet diverse.

***

Q5: What are the key qualities of a coach?

As an expert in individual coaching but not in team coaching, my answer will focus on coaches who work with individuals. Of course, many of the key qualities are applicable to both approaches, but if you want to know more about team coaching, I encourage you to look into the ORSC-training which specialises in coaching teams and other forms of partnership.

Rather than including a long list of coaching skills and tools, I'm taking a different approach to answering this question. For those who want to know all the tools, the *Co-Active Coaching* book is a great resource.

This book, like many other books and training programmes about coaching, will tell you all you need to know about the competencies for a professional coach. Coaching is a serious profession and your coachees deserve a well-trained coach. You've got to know what you are doing, which includes a solid ethical awareness.

I see three circles which capture the essence of what makes a good coach: Competence, Confidence and Authenticity.

It starts with just getting good at what you are doing from a technical perspective. Just go to coaching school and get the COMPETENCIES you need to become a professional coach.

The technique is important, yet it's not all! You need to believe that you know what you are doing. You need to step into CONFIDENCE and embrace being a professional. As much as you want your coachees to believe in their qualities, do the same yourself!

Competencies and Confidence, marinated in AUTHENTICITY, lead to magic and the more these circles overlap, the bigger the RANGE of the coach will be. Do not copy the textbook, nor another coach. As they say, be yourself, everyone else is taken. This is what you encourage your coachees to step into, so inspire them by practising what you're preaching.

Finally, you also want your coachees to know what it is to be an effective partner in this process: make sure there is CLARITY. You've got to be able to give the context your coachee needs to play their part of the game.

***

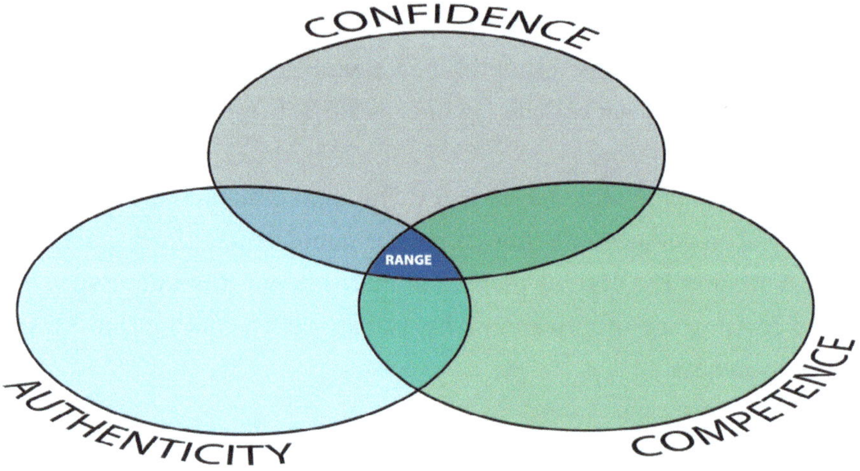

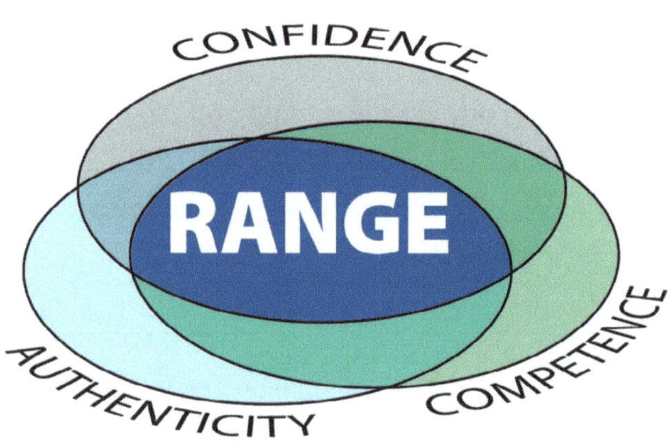

Q6: How to develop these qualities?

What makes a piano player a maestro, a violinist a virtuoso?

What made Rembrandt the master painter he was? What made Taylor Swift the great artist she is?

In addition to fully embracing the circles mentioned in the previous question, they have one more thing in common: they keep investing time, energy and money in PRACTISE!

Bryan Adams played his guitar till his fingers bled, practised until the skin on his fingers was hurting. Because he was passionate about playing the guitar and becoming really good at what he loves doing.

Besides practising, practising and practising (did I already mention practising?), ongoing education, always being open to and seeking to receive feedback, with a constant desire to be '1% better than yesterday', will make you the best version of a coach you can become.

For that, dear colleague, you need patience. This will not happen overnight. It takes time to become a master in whatever you are doing. To become a Master Coach, the ICF requires no less than 2,500 hours of experience. That's a lot of practise...

***

Q7: Can we coach our family and friends?

Many coaches have received the following feedback from their nearest and dearest: 'Stop coaching me'!

In all their enthusiasm for their newfound role, the coach is applying their amazing skills and tools to everyone they can get their hands on. With or without permission and forgetting to consciously design the relationship.

In general, we say it is not a good idea to coach people close to you. In a healthy coaching relationship, the coach is 100% neutral in what the coachee decides to do or not to do. That is possible because these decisions do not impact the coach's life. The coach can literally say: "Hey, it's up to you, it's your life after all".

No matter how strong the coach is self-managing their own thoughts, opinions and possible solutions, there's a fair chance some of that will 'slip through their fingers' and influence their questions and how they show up in the coaching. Additionally, in coaching, people share their deepest secrets, confess all their mistakes and show the naked truth. This is possible because the coach can treat all of that with respect and confidentiality, without an agenda regarding what needs to be done with that information. In most personal relationships, there is a limit to how much of these things we are comfortable sharing. And even if the coachee is free to do so, does the coach really want to know all of this about their friends, family, even their partner? You know, fairly often ignorance is bliss...

So I would say 'No' to coaching people you are close with. At the same time, many coaches have learned that coaching is more than a technique. It is also a way of being and a way of looking at people. Coaches learn to listen differently. Coaches ask different kinds of questions. Just to name a few examples of qualities we can apply anytime, anywhere. When we really listen to someone, relationships deepen. When we are really curious about what the other person wants, that friend, family member or partner, our questions change.

A coach-like lifestyle and way of being will grow any relationship. But we should let coaching be a professional and objective activity where the coach and the coachee can both feel free to show up fully.

***

Q8: How about coaching colleagues?

It's really amazing to see organisations increasingly invest in training some of their staff to become internal coaches. With that, they create an environment where their employees have easy access to the support of a coach. Amazing!

An internal coach needs to be extra aware of how to design a coaching relationship where it is possible for the coachee, who is also a colleague, to feel fully safe and to know they can rely on full confidentiality.

The rule of thumb is that it's not a smart idea to coach people with whom you are in a hierarchical relationship. No, that's not a smart thing to do at all! Today I share my struggles and frustrations with you as my coach, and tomorrow you need to decide on my promotion or raise? That's not clean and I would even say that's not ethical!

Another challenge is coaching a colleague who shares the same experiences as you or when the coach has specific knowledge of their environment. It can be really hard to self-manage and not to become a consultant and give advice. Maybe the coach can self-manage, but how is it for the coachee when they know their coach holds all that knowledge or experience? There is a fair chance that they will ask over and over again 'what would you do?'.

Internal coaching can work really well when there is no direct link between the coach and the coachee. When they work in a different branch or department. When the coach can be neutral and objective about what the coachee decides to do or not to do.

When an organisation is too small for this, it's probably better to hire an external coach.

***

Q9: How to design a coaching culture in an organisation?

Following up on the previous question, let's take a look at what it takes to create a coaching culture within an organisation. It's rather easy to find someone who wants to be trained, maybe even certified and accredited as a coach. Many organisations just do the maths and calculate the investment to train one, or a few coaches, versus what they would pay to hire an external coach. That makes sense, but it's definitely not the only thing to keep in mind when you want to instill a coaching culture!

Apart from the coach, we have the employees who will be the future coachees. There are the managers with ideas about what coaching is and how they feel about using it, or not. There is HR who has certain thoughts about it and, of course, also the leader of the organisation.

One thing is easy to predict: all stakeholders have a different perspective on what coaching is and why it would, or would not, work for the organisation in question. There will be supporters of the idea to make coaching available for the employees, there will be those who think it's a waste of time. There will be the silent group, who are undecided, or the colleagues who are the 'resistance under the surface'.

We can compare this with cultural change. These processes take time and need support from the top where leading by example is always the best way forward.

It takes COURAGE from the pioneers and they need to prepare for support, hesitancy and resistance. So they need to COMMUNICATE clearly about their vision, about WHY COACHING will benefit the organisation. If they're smart, they will start with CONVINCING the top and the best way to explain what coaching is, is to have someone experience it. After sharing best practises, as well as what it took to get there, from other organisations, the COMMITMENT from the top is needed.

It really takes time to create CLARITY about what coaching is, who will get it, why they will get it and how the processes will be designed. All of this needs to be laid out in a CONTRACT between the top and those who will lead this programme and become the internal coaches. An essential part of this contract is to be very clear about the CONFIDENTIALITY so people will feel safe to participate.

It's been proven to be very helpful to start with training the leaders and the managers on what coaching is, and teaching them some of the basic skills. There is a fair chance they will not become internal coaches, but when they understand and experience what coaching is, there's a much bigger chance they will support the idea. Additionally, they will benefit from what they've learned in their role as a manager, for instance. They will start asking different questions and they will listen in a different way. Basic coaching skills are a gift in every role we have in life, including a management role.

The processes need to be transparent, clear and available to all who will give or receive the coaching. An essential part of the process is to define the role of the coach, the coachee/employee and the sponsor/manager/HR. Who will give and receive which information? Who is responsible for what? Where and how to complain? How many sessions?

We could probably fill a whole book with the full answer to this question. Yet with this short reflection, you will have some of the key elements to keep in mind when introducing coaching in an organisation.

***

Q10: What are the limitations of coaching?

We can explore many different things in coaching and the range of topics I've seen over time is huge. I do not see a limit to which topics someone could bring up. Yes, there are (exceptional) situations involving ethical or legal boundaries that we need to keep in mind, but in general I'd say any topic is welcome. Though there is a limit to how we can support our coachees.

Maybe the additional question to ask is: for whom is coaching?

I have shared my answer to that question on the homepage of my website: *'Coaching is for well-functioning people, desiring to transform from good to great, consciously creating the life they really want'.*

This includes three key-ingredients:

- Well-functioning
- A longing to grow
- Conscious choice

We need to be able to look at our coachees as well-functioning human beings who can oversee the consequences of their choices. In Co-Active coaching we'd probably say that we must be able to see our coachee as 'Naturally Creative, Resourceful and Whole'. If we can't, I feel we should not coach this person and either refer them to another colleague or to a therapist.

When our coachee comes to coaching, but doesn't have a desire to grow, what's the point? Coaching is about change, transformation even. When the coachee is not able to move away from the status quo, or is stuck in the past and unable to free themselves from this, coaching is not what would serve them most at this point in time.

When a person is not able to make conscious choices, I see that as another red flag for coaching. I'm not talking about finding it hard, sometimes, to make such a choice. We all experience that. Yet when someone is so stuck in emotions, in the past or in Limiting Beliefs (see question 30) that they're not able to make choices to grow and live towards the life they're longing for, I would not be able to coach this person.

Sometimes it is really difficult for a coach to decide whether someone is coachable or not. Therefore it's important to have a network of respected colleagues and representatives from neighbouring professions that we can go to for advice. Without having to break confidentiality, we can discuss a case study and find wisdom on how to move forward.

***

Q11: How to choose our coachees?

Coaching is not a business where the coach should accept everyone because 'business is business'. Coaching is a 'relationship focused business', and both the potential coachee and the coach deserve a consciously chosen partnership. As referred to before, an essential part of coaching is the 'partnering'. If one of the two does not feel inspired by this relationship, how can we create that 'thought-provoking and creative process'?

The book *The Prosperous Coach* by Steve Chandler & Rich Litvin inspired me with their 'Hell Yes or Hell No' principle for selecting your future coachees. Both coach and coachee deserve to commit wholeheartedly to this new partnership.

An important resource to tap into as coaches is our intuition. During the chemistry session (aka introduction call), and even during the communication before that, our gut feeling will give us essential information about this possible partnership. Dare to trust this and even when you do not feel a 'Hell No' but a 'Maybe', let that be enough information. In that case, just be honest and trust that there's a better match waiting for both of you.

It is also essential to find out if the prospective coachee is clear about what coaching is and what it will ask from them. Often the person new to coaching only has some assumptions about what this process may look like. Are they looking for a coach or are they mixing up job titles and instead searching for a consultant? On more than one occasion, I've had interactions with people for whom the words coach, consultant and trainer meant more or less the same thing. Most people are used to working with some kind of specialist they consult to solve a specific problem. I am very grateful that these people exist and frequently work with them myself, but it is not the same as coaching. So: creating clarity and managing expectations is key.

Another filter to use, is how motivated the potential coachee is to embark on this journey. Have they been sent by their manager and are they here to please them? Do they feel obliged to work with a coach to fix a problem? Hmmm, alarm bells!

A surprise to some is that the coachee is actually going to do most of the work in the partnership and that the vast majority of this happens in between the sessions. If they're not willing to commit to that, the impact might be that the coach takes a responsibility which is not theirs to carry. The coach starts to work harder and harder to make sure the coachee will get something out of the coaching, and that is not in service of the coachee.

So these are the key things to keep in mind when choosing your coachees:

- Trust your gut feeling.
- Only say 'Yes' when it feels like a 'Hell Yes'!
- Create clarity and manage expectations.
- Find out more about the coachee's motivations.
- Make sure the potential coachee is willing to do the work.

***

Q12: What's important in marketing our services?

Many coaches struggle to promote their coaching services since they feel like they're selling themselves. Though they may have a background in marketing, where they were successfully selling products or services from the organisation they worked for, they get paralysed by their Saboteur when it comes to their own services. If I were their Saboteur, I would do the same! The Saboteur is allergic to change and since coaching is all about change, it's a super effective move from the Saboteur to stop the coach from evoking all this transformational change, even before they get started. 'Stop the change in the coach so they cannot call forth the change in their future coachees. Let's make them feel unworthy and incompetent and they will think twice before they start looking for coachees'.

If you recognise this, dear colleague, look that Saboteur in the eye and give yourself more reasons as to why coaching is more important to you than your Saboteur can think of reasons why it isn't!

How is coaching an expression of your 'Big Why'? What values are you honouring by coaching people? Questions like this will help you reconnect with the resonance you experienced when you were introduced to coaching. Find yourself someone who can coach you on this and grow stronger; make yourself unstoppable. The world needs you and your coaching services to make it a better place!

From here, keep the following marketing pillars in mind:

- Visibility
- Credibility
- Likeability

In your marketing activities, make sure the world knows that you exist and that you are available as a coach. Sharing this once on social media is not enough. You have to keep repeating the message so people start to connect the word 'coach' to your name. Give them a chance to get to know you!

Everything you communicate has an impact. Let what you say or write contribute to your credibility, to being seen as a reliable and professional coach. A key element here is the testimonials from your previous coachees. Either ask them for a written statement that you can share on your website, for instance, or inspire them to become your ambassadors. There's this expression that all you need to do is create 1,000 'raving fans' and they will do the marketing for you by word of mouth.

The third factor, likeability, is not a contest in who is the most popular coach! It is about giving yourself the permission to be real and authentic in how you show up, which includes your marketing. No, not all eight billion people will like you! Yet by being your wonderful self, your kind of people will find you. Give people a chance to get a feel for who and how you are through what you communicate in your marketing messages. Give the world a chance to get to like you!

***

Q13: What's a good marketing tool?

Making yourself visible requires specific, structured and repetitive action. For this, I found the *Get Clients Now!* approach, by CJ Hayden, very supportive. This programme has a run through time of four weeks, and you work on it five days per week. Since there are countless different ways to market ourselves, it first helps us to select a few filters through which we look at all the possible actions we could take. You set specific goals, clear intentions, and you even choose a little reward for yourself after the four weeks. You select ten clear and measurable actions that are going to help you achieve your goals. There is a built-in accountability structure so even when you do it completely alone, you always have a clear view on how things are evolving.

Have a look to see if this programme is something for you!

Many, many times I hear colleagues complain about not having enough coachees. I then ask them a few simple questions:
- "How many working hours a week do you have available?" Let's say this number is 40.
- "How many of them are you already spending on serving coachees?" Let's say this number is 15.
- "How many hours are filled with office work, product development or study?" Let's say this number is 5.

This means you have 40, minus 15, minus 5, which makes 20 hours left and these hours need to be dedicated to marketing your services. This is a very simple way to measure if you live up to the concept 'You are either serving a coachee or searching for one', which I learned from the book *The Prosperous Coach*.

As a little exercise, it might be a nice idea to take a look at what your answers are to these three questions and how many of the available hours for marketing you're actually using for this purpose?

After some time using the *Get Clients Now!* approach myself, I simplified it slightly. I created the 'Three Magical Circles' which I've shared in many workshops to support others in their marketing. The idea is simple:
Circle one is your inner circle. You probably don't want to coach the people in your inner circle, but they are your biggest fans.
Circle two includes the people you're rather familiar with but the relationship has enough distance, so you can objectively coach them. The people in this circle know and appreciate you.
Circle three includes the people in your network who you do not often engage with. You may have studied with them or worked together once upon a time. They are clearly far away enough for you to coach them, but they do already know your name.

Everyone outside these three circles is 'the rest of the world'. Since every person has these kinds of circles around them, in a magical way all of their circles and yours are connected. Inspired by the theory of the 'Six degrees of separation', I believe that all people are six or fewer social connections away from each other. This creates a chain of 'a friend of a friend' and when we activate our first three circles of friends, they can become your ambassadors and activate their circles. This makes the world your playground!

You can activate your three circles in a simple way.
1: Tell them what you do and what you are looking for.
2: Ask them if they want to look in their environment if they know someone who's interested in coaching.
3: Ask those in circles two and three if they themselves are interested in coaching.
4: Each week, choose five names from each circle and reach out to them.
5: The next week, follow up with them, and choose five new names from each circle and repeat the steps above.

Try this for a month and don't be surprised if you start to see things moving!

***

Q14: What if we're being ghosted by a coachee?

Okay, here is my confession. One of the more frustrating things that can happen to me as a coach is being ghosted by the coachee. Or a potential coachee with whom I had an introduction call (aka Chemistry call). Let me share two examples.

After working for a rather long time with a coachee, she cancelled the last calls very last minute, or just didn't show up for the call. Me waiting on Zoom, nobody joining the waiting room. Since she was always on time for the calls, after waiting for five minutes, I sent a message asking if everything was okay and if she could join the call. No response. Nothing. More waiting. After 15 minutes, I decided to leave the call and sent one more message letting her know that I had left Zoom and asking if she was still able to join for the remainder of the call. Still no response and this leaves you wondering what's happening? Familiar with that feeling?

In the days after, still nothing.

For the next call, the last one scheduled in this agreement, I received a very short message right before the call stating that she was not able to make it. After that, radio-silence. Despite a few mails to check in, nothing. Ghosted!

The other example is a wonderful person with whom I had an inspiring chemistry call. We both felt this was a 'Hell Yes' and all that needed to be sorted was some administrative stuff. After sharing all the paperwork, as we agreed, and a link to start scheduling the sessions, nothing. The next sign of life from him was that he posted on the same platform as where we found each other, that he was looking for a coach... Again, ghosted! Of course someone can change their mind, but I would greatly appreciate it if this were communicated.

Though I'm a big boy and know that things sometimes go differently from what I expect or hope, it always leaves me with a feeling that my time has not been respected by the other person. What to do? How to treat this annoying experience?

Whilst reflecting on this question, at some point I found myself with the Co-Active Model in my hands. I was staring at it, looking at the different components of the model and wondering where I would find an answer? Three things caught my eye: Curiosity, Self-Management and Designing The Alliance. Over and over I need to be reminded that curiosity is the antidote to judgement! It happens so fast – especially when I'm being ghosted – that I find myself slipping into judgement. I start to blame the other person. Oops, I did it again...! What if I, instead of allowing myself to have all kinds of negative thoughts and feeling sorry for myself, replaced that with genuine curiosity? What if I wondered what is going on for this person that makes it not possible for them to join a call or to respond to messages? How about if I assumed good intent? Or asked myself what the lesson in this situation is, or reflected on where I show similar behaviour? Hmm, this will not only keep me busy with myself rather than with the other person for a while, but this might also teach me some important lessons that I need to learn.

This does take some self-management: it takes a conscious choice to look at this situation in a different way. As we often say when we talk about 'Perspectives': 'the way you look at something defines what you see and how you feel about it'.

I have a choice! I cannot decide how the world is treating me, yet I can decide how I look at what is happening. I am not a victim and 'poor me, poor me' never helped me connect with my authentic, most powerful self. I can choose how I will allow my mood to be influenced by situations like these. I have a choice of how I use the time that just became available. An example of what I've learned that helps me is the following: Let's say a coachee is not showing up for a call and it needs to be counted as a missed session. After the waiting and the messaging, that usually leaves me with 30 minutes or so that I can use for other purposes. I always have things to do that do not excite me, but they just need to happen. I use the 'Pomodoro-principle' and commit 25 minutes of focused time to these tasks, followed by five minutes of free time. Not so exciting tasks suddenly become a paid activity 😊

Linked to curiosity and assuming good intent, self-management also influences the words and tone I choose when communicating with the person involved. It's not that hard to choose to start the message with something really kind. Ask instead of tell. Leave an opening for them to come back without having to walk the walk of shame. Treat them as you, as I, would like to be treated when I mess up. Before hitting the 'Send-button', re-read the message and look at the words through the filter 'Was it kind, was it necessary?'. And if you feel there's still some kind of emotion, don't hit that 'Send-button' yet, because you will probably regret what you're about to communicate. If needed, just wait till the next day since the night puts many things in a different light.

Designing the Alliance, thus, probably starts with ourselves. What do I need to design with myself in how I choose to show up in situations like this? The most important relationship we have in life, after all, is the one with ourselves. Am I able to look myself in the eye in the bathroom mirror in the evening and say "You did the right thing"? Should I avoid looking into my own eyes, knowing I didn't honour my own standards, simply justified by someone else not honouring theirs? I know this is a rhetorical question, but still worthwhile asking.

Of course, Designing the Alliance is also applicable to each coaching relationship, the ones already existing or just about to start.

I've learned to ask coachees at the end of a chemistry call to always let me know what they've decided, even when it's a 'no'. The context I give is that I can then close this chapter for myself and delete the information they may have shared out of privacy considerations. This approach seriously reduced the number of times I've been ghosted by a potential new coachee. And if they still choose to not communicate, I have curiosity and self-management to lean into. In an existing, ongoing coaching relationship, I also address things clearly in the contract I have with my coachees. And by having all calls scheduled in advance and paid upfront, the number of 'no-shows' or being ghosted is seriously reduced. We design the agreement in a transparent way where we also mention that the last scheduled session for this agreement is used for Evaluation. And again, if the ghosting then happens, back to curiosity and self-management.

For me, the conclusion to this question is that real ghosting only happens when I ghost my own values and do not show up in the way I'd like to.

What is your conclusion?

***

Q15: What about AI and coaching?

Great question! For a moment I thought this meant 'Alex Intelligence' but then my wonderful son told me what it really stands for, making his 'old man' aware that there are things he could be a bit more curious about. Joking aside, with things like this I certainly don't fall into the category of 'early adopters' and I take my time, to see where this is going.

A quote from Harvard Business School Professor Karim R. Lakhani that really inspired me to take a closer look at this topic: *'AI won't replace humans – But humans with AI will replace humans without AI'.*

I personally believe that the relationship between coach and coachee forms a big part of the magic in coaching. We include everything that our coachee is communicating: communication is where we perceive our coachee as a whole person. Not only their words, but also the way they say them, the pauses, the silences. Their gestures and facial expressions. The look in their eyes. Their watering eyes. And I could go on listing various things that make me think, "Good luck capturing that, AI!".

But I cannot and will not deny that Artificial Intelligence can also support professions which are primarily based on human relationships.

Since there are many different perspectives on this topic, and I believe they all hold some truth and wisdom, I asked colleagues how they feel about AI in our profession. Are you 'In Favour', are you 'Against' or do you feel 'Ambivalent'? They were asked to explain their perspective in 200-300 words and below you will find short contributions from each of these categories. I've also asked ChatGPT what it had to say about each of these perspectives and included that below the other answers. Hey, humans first 😉

By the way, those three parts are the only ones in the book written by ChatGPT. To be fair, for some questions I did do some additional research on the internet. In a way, this is just a different method of using the collective knowledge given to us through a machine...

***

Q16: Why should AI be a part of the future of coaching?

Here are the contributions of those who volunteered to share their 'In Favour' perspective, followed by the answer ChatGPT gave to this question.

As a long-time career and life coach, an author, and a content creator, I initially resisted using AI for anything. It was like joining the evil empire that profits from siphoning originality from the masses. This is an ethical issue that remains to be considered.

On a practical level, what changed my mind about using AI in coaching is that generators such as ChatGPT and Gemini do provide relevant information quickly, especially for brainstorming and 'raw', unfiltered insight.

The unknown or ambiguity is unnerving to most people. Employing AI to make suggestions, outline how-to's, derive raw answers involving multiple disciplines helps to quell some of the anxiety and give room for exploration (e.g. Name career options for a second grade teacher who loves to make pottery, write, and encourage people. Or how can a recent college grad save for a house in 5 years?).

AI is a tool for coaching, not a replacement. It is a supplement. The coach guides, asks empowering questions to get the client to interact with the data from AI, to discern their values, feelings, and sense of possibilities. We facilitate self-understanding and resonance in the process.

Often people come to coaching because they are lost, unhappy, scared, and needing structure to build their confidence and agency. Coaches champion clients' causes, provide context, and help them uncover their inner resources for a tangible shift. Knowledge and collective perspectives summarised by AI can help with this.

AI will not replace a human coach who has intuition and energetic connection to a client. There is a place for it in coaching. And like any powerful tool, we need to know how to use it.

By Sue Wang, CPCC, PCC, EdM, Career & Life Coach, Author

- - -

As a coach I cannot deny the need for connection and intimacy in a coaching session. AI is not here to create that for us. AI is more like a companion, a co-lead in the journey of coaching. Often as coaches we incur repetitive work and sometimes we need to educate our coachees in certain terms and this is something that we can easily delegate to AI. Yet, up until now the efforts of developing an AI that can create the level of intimacy a human being can, haven't yielded many results. There are different types of AI: in our era we have been able to develop up until what's called Generative AI and there are efforts to develop the Super AI, where the biggest difference is how one is closer to the human experience. Generative AI is definitely a good co-lead in identifying habits and exploring perspectives. Super AI has been a little slower to develop because it needs more information on how we develop in our human experience. So far there is not much data on how a baby from being a newborn, experiences every single day and how the different variables affect the way that humans developed the intelligence and ability to relate. Only if we could find a way to connect all of our consciousness in a readable way, would we be able to create a super AI that might mimic the ability of a human being to relate. But until we can connect as humans in our reality, the dream of having a super AI that can relate as a human is far from becoming real.

By Denisse Eugenia Vega Aguirre, CPCC, PCC, ICP-ENT, ORSC

- - -

In professional development, the synergy between human coaching and artificial intelligence (AI) presents exciting opportunities. While a coach's role as a professional human thinking partner remains irreplaceable, AI can significantly enhance the coaching process when used responsibly.

AI's analytical capabilities offer a powerful complement to human coaching. For instance, when presented with a coachee's detailed portfolio of achievements, skills, and capabilities, AI can instantly conduct a comprehensive analysis, identifying skill gaps and key strengths that might take a human coach considerably longer.

Furthermore, AI excels at ideation, particularly in exploring career paths. It can suggest not only logical progressions from a current career but also innovative options based on transferable skills, potentially opening doors the coachee hadn't considered.

Another promising application is scenario simulation. As coachees contemplate various paths forward, AI can model potential outcomes, providing a data-driven foundation for decision-making.

However, the key to harnessing AI's potential in coaching lies in adopting the right approach. First, AI should be viewed as a powerful tool, not a replacement for human judgment. The emotional intelligence of a human coach remains crucial.

Secondly, an ethical approach is paramount. AI should never be used to misrepresent a person's true identity or capabilities. It should only enhance the authentic presentation of a coachee's skills and potential.

The most effective results will emerge from a tripartite partnership: a coachee driving their own development, a human coach providing insights and guidance, and AI responsibly employed for analytics and ideation.

By Anastasia Mizitova, SHRM-SCP, CPCC, CEO of Talent14

\- - -

AI should be a part of the future of coaching for several reasons:

1. ***Personalization:*** *AI can analyze individual behaviour, preferences, and progress, allowing for customised coaching plans that cater to the unique needs of each client.*
2. ***Data Analysis:*** *AI can handle large volumes of data, providing insights and identifying patterns that human coaches might miss. This can help in tracking progress and adjusting strategies effectively.*
3. ***Accessibility:*** *AI-driven coaching tools can provide support at any time and from anywhere, making coaching more accessible to a wider range of people, including those who may not afford traditional coaching.*
4. ***Scalability:*** *AI can support multiple clients simultaneously, allowing coaches to extend their services to more people without diminishing the quality of coaching.*
5. ***Continuous Improvement:*** *AI systems can learn and evolve, becoming more effective over time as they gather more data and feedback from users.*
6. ***Cost-Effectiveness:*** *AI solutions can reduce costs associated with traditional coaching methods, making coaching available to more individuals and organizations.*
7. ***Enhanced Engagement:*** *AI can incorporate gamification and interactive elements, making the coaching experience more engaging and motivating for clients.*
8. ***Objective Feedback:*** *AI can provide unbiased feedback based on data rather than personal opinions, helping clients see areas for improvement more clearly.*

Integrating AI into coaching can enhance the overall effectiveness of coaching practices, support growth, and help individuals achieve their goals more efficiently.

By ChatGPT

***

Q17: Why should AI not be a part of the future of coaching?

Here are the contributions of those who volunteered to share their 'Against' perspective, followed by the answer ChatGPT gave to this question.

Coaching is about making connections and empowering those connections to make positive changes through meaningful dialogues and discussions. If we look back, we would understand that the progress of humanity (or human evolution) can be attributed to its superpower of making tribes through connections. "Human species", by bonding together, thrived and achieved unprecedented growth throughout history. And if we dig deep, we would also realise that any human tie is basically the manifestation of emotional connections. Magic happens when you connect at the emotional level and you cooperate to make things better.

However, in today's world, we have become more obsessed with materialistic possessions and less available emotionally to make connections that enrich our existence. If just having social media was not enough, the advent of AI has rocked the very foundational belief of humanity's progress.

AI threatens very basic human rights – privacy and confidentiality. AI also brings an unfathomable amount of bias and prejudice into the system, which at any coaching discussion is against the ethics and principles of the practice. Bringing AI into coaching also means that we are just data, for someone else, and our human adventures and misadventures are not our personal and unique experiences anymore.

We are in the age of the "loneliness epidemic", and while some people might be tempted to use AI as their "coach" for the sheer easiness of finding some kind of advice, it would eventually be like using self-prescription drugs for all of life's struggles and issues, big or small, without understanding the root cause of the unwell-being. Eventually, that disconnect from reality will create more loneliness, frustration, anger and resentment in society. And we, coaches, as the torch-bearers of well-being, must raise our voices and concerns against this.

By Pritam Jha, CPCC, ACC

- - -

I assume that all AI coaching algorithms are geared to follow and learn about an individual's preferences and take note of their likes and dislikes. Then, content is filtered according to the customer's preference.

Examples include Target's algorithm to identify the purchase preferences of women as they discover that they are pregnant, then gear all merchandising to support a new mother. Or Facebook's algorithm to identify your preferences and gear the content to support that.

This would be in vogue, with the majority of AI algorithms set out to track and process customer information.

AI, operating in a binary world, can overlook the intricate shades of grey and the vast nuances that exist in every human interaction. This stark limitation underscores the irreplaceable need for human intervention in coaching, highlighting the significant role that human coaches play in the coaching process.

A human being has the capacity to draw from our five senses: seeing, hearing, feeling, smelling and tasting, plus a sixth sense of intuition. In this sense, humans can work with more data points or a six-dimensional versus a two-dimensional reference point.

The potential for an AI program to beat the world's best chess players is evident as the computer can process an infinite number of future possibilities and is gearing itself to answer those challenges, which is Level 1 Listening.

Unlike AI, a human coach possesses the unique ability to be fully present in the moment, connecting to all six senses at Level 3 Listening. This deep connection allows them to be genuinely curious and explore the content of what is being said, while holding the client's agenda and desired outcome in high regard. This emotional resonance, a unique aspect of human coaching, is something that AI, with all its algorithms, cannot replicate.

By David Bingley CPCC, PCC. Founder In-Vision Coaching

- - -

While there are many benefits to incorporating AI into coaching, there are also several reasons why it may not be suitable:

1. ***Lack of Human Connection:*** *Coaching often relies on interpersonal dynamics, empathy, and emotional intelligence, which AI may struggle to replicate. The human connection can be critical for building trust and rapport with clients.*
2. ***Understanding Nuance:*** *AI may have difficulty grasping the nuances of human behaviour, emotions, and complex situations that require a deeper understanding than data analysis can provide.*
3. ***Personalised Insight Limitations:*** *While AI can provide data-driven insights, it may not always consider individual life experiences, cultural contexts, or subjective factors that a human coach would recognise.*
4. ***Ethical Concerns:*** *The reliance on AI in coaching may raise ethical questions regarding data privacy, consent, and the potential for bias in algorithms impacting outcomes.*
5. ***Over-reliance on Technology:*** *Coachees may become overly reliant on AI-driven tools at the expense of developing their own critical thinking and problem-solving skills.*
6. ***Resistance to AI Solutions:*** *Some individuals may feel uncomfortable or wary of AI coaching, preferring the human touch and expertise that traditional coaching provides.*

7. ***Limited Adaptability:*** *AI systems may struggle to adapt to unexpected changes or complex emotional situations that require intuition and creativity, which are often important in coaching.*
8. ***Quality and Accountability Issues:*** *The quality of AI-driven coaching can vary significantly, and there may be challenges in holding AI accountable for negative outcomes or issues that arise during the coaching process.*

Overall, while AI can enhance certain aspects of coaching, it should not fully replace the valuable human skills and relationships that are integral to effective coaching. A balanced approach that combines AI technology with human expertise may be the most effective way forward.

By ChatGPT

***

Q18: What if we are ambivalent if AI should be a part of the future of coaching?

Here are the contributions of those who volunteered to share their 'Ambivalent' perspective, followed by the answer ChatGPT gave to this question.

AI coaching is a choice. It's the middle path between going it alone (with books and YouTube videos) and hiring a human guide. A customised journey without the hefty price tag.

But here's the thing: AI can mimic empathy, dispense wisdom, and meet you where you are. It can digest the sum wisdom of humankind and customise it to exactly what you personally need – a bespoke, on-demand trainer. AI coaching is getting more empathic every day. Soon, you might not even notice the difference between the way it talks and the way a human talks.

Yet, there's a gap. A chasm of accountability. We're social creatures, wired for connection. And as long as we see AI as not human, we'll struggle to commit. It's too easy to ignore, to dismiss, to hit snooze on our growth. Like how it's easy for people (like me) to hit the snooze repeatedly each morning. There are no emotional consequences to ignoring an AI coach, and hence, it is so much easier to avoid the painful, awkward places where growth happens. So much of growth is accepting frustration and doing things anyways.

For some, AI coaches will be perfect. New tricks for old tasks.

For others, those needing a gentle push from the nest, the accountability gap looms large. It's hard to leave the bird nest when your mama bird is just a robot mama – when the experience feels inauthentic.

The question isn't whether AI coaching works. It's whether it works for you.

By Chris Tran, CPCC
Helping Gaming Professionals Everywhere

- - -

Regardless of our feelings towards it, AI has embedded itself, most likely forever more, into our homes, workplaces, relationships, societies.

Some of us are scared that it will replace us and choose to run from it.

Some of us are in denial, digging our heads, ostrich-like, in the sand and choose to pretend it's not happening.

Some of us cheer from the rafters at the innovation and choose to embrace it.

Many of us – me included – have experienced all of these states of mind at various points over recent years.

Now, I choose acceptance.

I think of the cornerstones of Co-Active coaching and I feel the fear dissolve. Human connection is at the core and the Co-Active experience for the coach and coachee is uniquely human. It will never be replaced by AI. Then I think of the administrative side of running my coaching business and how AI supports me and I'm part of the cheer squad. AI saves me multiple hours every week, giving me the gift of extra time to spend on more coaching and learning. AI in coaching is not a battle of human versus AI. It is not a zero-sum game. The two co-exist and when we reach a place of acceptance, infinite opportunities open up.

By Aisling Gray
Coach and Communications Consultant

\- - -

If you are ambivalent about whether AI should be a part of the future of coaching, it's important to consider several factors to help clarify your thoughts and feelings on the subject:

1. ***Evaluate the Benefits and Drawbacks:*** *Make a list of the advantages and disadvantages. This can help you visualise both sides and recognise the aspects that matter most to you.*
2. ***Consider Hybrid Models:*** *Many coaching scenarios could benefit from a hybrid approach, where AI tools complement human coaches. This combination could leverage data-driven insights while preserving the essential human elements of empathy and connection.*
3. ***Reflect on Personal Values:*** *Consider your values regarding technology, human interaction, and the importance of emotional intelligence in coaching.*
4. ***Stay Informed:*** *Research the latest developments in AI and coaching. Understanding how AI is currently being used, and what ethical guidelines and best practices are emerging, can inform your opinion.*
5. ***Assess User Experiences:*** *Look into case studies or testimonials from individuals who have used AI coaching solutions. These first-hand accounts can provide valuable insights into effectiveness, satisfaction, and the overall experience.*
6. ***Engage in Discussions:*** *Talk with coaches, coachees, or experts in the field to gain diverse perspectives on the integration of AI.*

7. ***Pilot Programs:*** *If possible, consider engaging with AI coaching tools in a trial capacity to experience firsthand their capabilities and limitations.*
8. ***Consider Long-Term Implications:*** *Think about the future landscape of coaching and how AI may evolve. Reflect on how technological advancements may change the nature of coaching and what that means for human coaches and coachees.*

Ultimately, ambivalence is a natural response to the rapid changes technology brings. Exploring your thoughts and engage with the topic can lead to a more informed and balanced perspective on the role of AI in the future of coaching.

By ChatGPT

***

Q19: How is it to live with two coaches in one house?

Time for a fun question from the wide variety of questions I've received. This one definitely made me smile! In a previous answer, I referred to how challenging it can be to live with an enthusiastic coach who wants to coach you at any given time, whether you asked for it or not. This question adds another layer, and I gladly dive into this question since I believe having two coaches in one house can be both a blessing as well as an even bigger challenge...

Coaching requires a certain distancing from the topic the coachee brings to the table. When both partners are trained as a coach, this can for sure help them to self-manage and look at the bigger picture. I tend to believe that coaches find it somewhat easier to respond consciously rather than react from an angle driven by emotions. (Note to self: try to remember this more often...)

When partners go through a challenging time, and when they're both trained coaches, they can choose to use certain exercises in their attempt to deal with their issues. From a personal perspective, I can share that this helped my marriage to overcome things that otherwise could have had a huge, lasting, negative impact on the relationship.

So, when both partners are ready and willing to choose to lean into their skills and their state of being as a coach, it can for sure have a positive impact on their relationship.

I can imagine, however, that being too 'coach-like' at certain points in time can annoy the hell out of your partner.

When I have one of my famous clumsy moments and hurt myself again, all I need is a partner who gives me a band-aid and who does not ask the very popular coaching question "Where do you feel this in your body"... And when it really hurts badly, who puts an arm around me and comforts me.

At other moments, I don't want my emotions to be explored in a professional coaching way, I just want to be sad, frustrated or angry. Unreasonable even (confession 😉).

My wife, who is also a CPCC, is wise enough to just leave me alone in those moments and to wait until later to check with me if I need something from her.

I'm sure you can think of various situations where you don't want to be coached, you just want to be your excited or disappointed, sad or silly, happy or frustrated self. I think it is, in a certain way, healthy to allow raw emotions to just be. And only when both coach-partners are ready and willing to use another approach, could a coaching-related method be chosen. But each partner should have the freedom to not step into the coaching role. It might be asking too much of them when there's too much personal emotional involvement.

This is why each coach deserves their own coach, even when they're sleeping next to one.

***

Q20: Why should we join the ICF?

The International Coaching Federation (ICF) was founded in 1995 and over time, it has become the world's largest organisation of professionally trained coaches, and the leading voice for the global coaching community. Like any young organisation, it went through several phases of development before growing into its current role.

Since 2021, it introduced a new ICF brand and the ICF ecosystem, which reflects ICF's interests in many areas of the coaching industry, represented by six unique family organisations. If you want to read more about this, have a look at the website which holds tons of information about how the ICF can serve and grow the coaching profession.

This is what the ICF is, yet why join? For me the main answer is: a shared responsibility to grow our profession to higher standards. Though never underestimating the impact of our individual actions, collectively we are so much stronger! I am convinced that the ICF played a very important role in putting coaching 'on the map'. The gift for the individual coach is that most organisations now take coaching seriously and see it as an important tool to support the growth of their employees.

In simple terms, without the ICF's 25+ years of hard work, coaching would not be as widely accepted, and we would have far fewer opportunities to coach and earn a living..

Another advantage I see is the credentialling the ICF offers. Whether you are an ACC, a PCC or an MCC, your title certainly says something about how serious you take your profession. More and more organisations include this in their selection criteria so without these credentials, you would not be considered to coach within their organisation.

Furthermore, I want to point out that we can look at our profession as a self-regulating system. The ICF Code of Ethics – and the professional coaches respecting it – is one of the reasons why there are hardly any countries with specific laws about coaching. Something to be proud of and to protect!

There's much more to say about the ICF, but if you're really curious about it, take a peek at its website.

Is there nothing critical to be said about the ICF then? Of course there is – for me personally, there are two things I'd like to see differently:
- There is so much information on its website that it can feel challenging to find your way. A more user-friendly website would be a blessing.
- The membership fee is perceived as rather high by many coaches. In addition to the annual membership fee, you must also pay every three years to renew your credentials. The amounts charged are the reason why some coaches let go of the membership or the credentials.

And finally, the ICF is the best-known coaching organisation in the world, but it is not the only one. Several countries have their own organisations and internationally, another respected organisation is called the 'Association for Coaching'.

***

Q21: What do you wish you had known when you started out as a coach?

Wow, I had to think about this question for a while... At first, all kinds of 'technical' things came up. For example, it would have been wonderful to understand how much more I could have done with my time if I had had the blessing of a PA from the beginning. Or embraced tools like Calendly much earlier to make life simpler and more efficient. Or learned additional techniques to expand my range to serve my coachees even better.

But I felt that wasn't the real answer. It isn't about more, smarter, or more efficient.

I wrote this text on a small piece of paper whilst staring out over the sea surrounding the island of Dugi Otok in Croatia. Sitting on a chair I found right next to the sea. Sometimes the waves even touched its legs and I had to pull up my feet to avoid getting my shoes wet. Of course, in moments like that I had to give up the writing. Try pulling up your feet and writing at the same time...

This is where and when I found the answer to this question. Only when I stopped pulling up my feet and accepted that the water wanted to touch me from time to time, could I continue writing. When I stopped trying to control the elements, I got into a flow. This is when I felt so alive and at one with the elements. Surrendering into the flow of things, rather than trying to control everything.

I looked out over the sea and saw dolphins jumping out of the water, playing. I felt at one with them because we both shared the same water. I could not stop watching them play.

So beautiful, so free.

The dolphins had a message for me. They do not worry nor try to control the circumstances. Why do I try so hard...?

I looked out over the water. In silence.
I looked up into the skies. In silence.
In silence I prayed*:

God, grant me the ***Serenity*** *to accept the things I cannot change,* ***Courage*** *to change the things I can, and* ***Wisdom*** *to know the difference.*

That serenity, that courage, that wisdom, I wish I could have had, all those years ago.

(* The AA version of *The Serenity Prayer*, originally written by Reinhold Niebuhr)

***

Q22: If you weren't a coach, which profession would you choose?

A firefighter saving lives every day? Professional hunter in Africa and be in nature from dawn to dusk? Or a policeman driving these really big, black cars with their blue flashing lights, fighting their way through traffic? Or one of the other cool jobs I dreamt about as a little boy. Okay, sometimes also as a big boy 😉

Looking at this list, I started off my career completely on the wrong foot. I left school at the age of 15, not knowing what to do with my life. Well, who does at that age...?

My father was a postman and I spent lots of time with him at the post office. The people behind the counters, responsible for lots of money and other seemingly important things, were the ones I thought were really important people. They made it. They were something my father could only dream of.

Long story short, with his help, I was accepted to be trained as one of these office clerks. What I didn't realise is that in essence I was trained to be responsible, serious and eventually get ready for a rather boring job. Bummer, wrong choice!

At the age of 18 I had to serve in the Dutch army for a while where they decided to make me a sergeant. In that role I felt a new kind of responsibility: for two groups of people who both were deeply frustrated with their job. One group was the soldiers who also had to be there, forced by law. The other group was the professionals who got promoted to their maximum level of boredom. Being the linking pin between these two groups sparked something in me. An interest in people and what makes them tick. After I did my service, I went back to the post office but I knew I had to work on getting out of there as soon as possible! Without higher education, I didn't have many opportunities back then, that's at least how I felt about it, so I went back to school alongside my full-time job. Three years at first, followed by another two to become an HR professional. Then another two to study management science. And I found the jobs and the income I aimed for. To eventually leave them for something I was passionate about and enabled me to travel the world, meet inspiring people and live many great adventures.

In hindsight, that is where I discovered three of my core values: adventure, taking risks and travelling the world – values that are integral to my sense of freedom. And there was a fourth one that I felt deep inside of me: making the world a slightly better place by building bridges between cultures, between people. From there, I discovered a fifth one: making people aware of what makes them thrive, and inspiring and supporting them to make that happen.

With coaching and training other coaches, I found myself in a really good place. And after trying out several other jobs, I finally found the confidence that I'm doing something I'm good at and that I love doing. This is something that gives me peace of mind. I'm at home in what I do. And if I were forced to change my professional activity at this point in life, I would look for something that ticks these boxes again. Indeed, the examples mentioned in the beginning would not meet these criteria.

But something else would. I would start a school, together with my wife, somewhere in the world where the children aren't born with a silver spoon in their mouth. My love for nature and adventure would take me to Africa. I would build us a simple house, next to the place where we would teach those children to get in touch with their talents and dreams. To explore and utilise these talents and dreams in a playful way, to avoid falling into the trap of becoming a boring adult. Teach them how to communicate in a non-violent way and learn what it is to create a life where no one gets rich by exploiting others. The young adults leaving that school would be value driven leaders, stepping into the world and paying forward. Collectively they would become an 'army of positive change'. Those who know about my Big Why will recognise these words. Because at the end of the day it's not that important what I do with my time and talents, as long as it's something that I'm passionate about. As long as I create a legacy that brings a smile to my face, I'm happy.

I have an image of my wife and I sitting on the porch and seeing these young ones spread their wings and fly out of the safe nest we offered them, our hearts filled with pride and love. See, there goes another one, making the world a bit of a better place. Holding them in our hearts for the rest of our life.

My job title? Ask them, when you meet them years after they leave the school.

***

Q23: What's the biggest mistake you've made as a coach?

Oops, confession time!

In all honesty, I don't keep a 'Top 3 mistakes' list, but certain situations come to mind. Let me give you some examples.

In my early days, I didn't get what it meant to set context in a supportive way for the coachee. Yes, we need to help them so they can play their part of the game. For example, working with concepts like someone's 'Big Why' (aka Life Purpose) or 'Inner Resources' often deserves some context setting. Without that, the coachee usually will not grasp the gift in this and it will have a counterproductive impact.

When I was explaining the whole Co-Active model to them, I for sure overdid it and the coachee was really wondering why they had to know all that...?

Another example was when I didn't reschedule a session, though I was way too tired to be fully present with my coachee. I probably didn't practise enough self-care and with that, my self-management slipped through my fingers. The lesson learned is to prioritise self-care. And when I can't be fully present, I reschedule the session.

At other times, 'the need' to get clients became more important than trusting my gut feeling. I felt we weren't able to both say 'Hell Yes!' to this coaching relationship, but I didn't listen to it. Though the temptation to accept any potential coachee can be big, I learned 'Maybe' equals 'Hell No' and I then trust that there's a better match for both of us out there.

When one thing leads to another after being hired by an organisation, for instance to do a workshop with one of their teams. Everyone is happy and the workshop is a success. During the evaluation with the CEO, the idea comes up to use the results of the workshop as the starting point for coaching some of the team members.

The line of confidentiality then easily becomes blurry, which of course has a negative impact on how safe the coachee feels. Even with the best design and pure intentions from both the CEO and the coach, the coachee might still question those intentions, often without saying so explicitly. This leads to them not fully opening up and keeping the handbrake on whilst being coached. Lesson: Keep the lines very clear and think twice before accepting multiple roles in one organisation.

The last one is about coaching for free. Many of us do it and it says something about how generous coaches often are. The question to ask though is: Why does it need to be for free and what are the terms?

Frequently the answer to the first question is that the coach doesn't dare to step into the professional self-confidence to charge a reasonable fee for their services. This is not the best way to establish an empowering coaching relationship. Additionally, I've learned that some people simply try to always get a bargain. Or that everything is open to negotiation. I had to learn to really get curious about why the coaching needs to be for free, or less than your regular fee.

When there's a good reason to coach someone for free, the 'Designed Alliance' (see question 50) requires some additional agreements. In too many cases I've experienced that when coaching is for free, it's not taken as seriously by the coachee. An example is frequent rescheduling at late notice, or even not showing up for a session. If we let them do that without any consequences, the time of the coach can become the 'flexible end' in the agenda of the coachee. With time being one of the most precious things in life and knowing a wasted hour cannot be replaced, I've learned to defend my time, even in these types of relationships. The deal is that I coach you for free, but when you mess with my time, I will charge you my full fee for that wasted session.

The lesson I had to learn was to take a stand for my time as an irreplaceable resource.

***

Q24: Why do coaches intrude and what tips do you have for intruding?

Many of us struggle with the skill of intruding – interrupting our coachee. There may be personal or cultural reasons why this is perceived as rude. And I get that, because under some circumstances intruding is simply not done.

So the first thing to look into, is what our personal relationship with intruding is. Which norm or value is being challenged when we intrude? We need to have an honest conversation with ourselves about this to understand our hesitations better.

From there, it's helpful to make a distinction between intruding in day-to-day life and intruding in coaching. Where in one context it may be rude to intrude, in coaching it might be rude not to.

For this we need to go back to the reason why we have this essential skill. Our coachees come to coaching to explore new terrain and not to explain to us what they already know. The old stories, all the details and data-dumping, are just tricks from their Saboteurs to keep them away from looking into new stories, new perspectives, new reasons to do or not to do something.

This can be used as context that we share with our coachee to explain why we may intrude at times. The first Golden Rule for Coaching in my previous book is: "Coaching is about exploration, not about explanation".

This is a quote I share with them, and we talk about how the need for intruding can become a part of our Designed Alliance, intended to support them to avoid explaining the details, the story they already know. I've never met a coachee that didn't agree with that, they want to get value for money after all.

The next time they fall back into explaining, all it takes is a simple reminder, asking them if they're explaining or exploring?

The rudeness is gone, the richness is there.

***

Q25: Coaching or therapy?

A variety of questions came in about coaching versus therapy:

- What's the difference?
- When does one need therapy instead of coaching?
- I've had therapy for years, why would coaching help me?

In the early days of coaching, the distinction may have been clearer. To bottom-line it, and I accept it's a very limited perspective, therapy focused on past traumas, while coaching focused on making choices for the future. Just to simplify it.

With time, the professions started to appreciate more and more of each other's tools and techniques. This created an overlap between the two professions, which doesn't make it easy to be clear about the differences.

For example, I've been working with Rachel, a psychologist, for a while with the intention, amongst other things, to understand why I'm responding in a certain way under specific circumstances. I noticed that several techniques Rachel used were very similar to what coaches use. Though she offered some specialised resources for me to explore, she didn't show up as the expert and didn't once give me the feeling of being her 'patient'.

But coaches can also choose to offer external resources sometimes, like books or exercises, to look into. A difference I notice between the two, apparently similar approaches, is that one is used to restore and heal, the other to expand and create. What I also observed, is that with Rachel's guidance, we frequently looked into things from the past to help me process these experiences.

An example of a technique Co-Active coaches are using and that clearly comes from the world of therapy, is what's known as 'Leader Within & Allies'. We all have multiple 'selves' and a way to get them to speak is through 'Voice Dialogue'. If you're interested, lots more information is available online.

In addition to Rachel's approach with me, some therapists choose a different approach. Where they step into the role of the expert, using techniques to help their patients (or clients), for instance to support them after they've experienced trauma. When there's something that needs healing, a cure.

This is clearly not what coaches are trained for and if we tried to do this, we would cross an ethical boundary.

After going through a process of healing, people often start working with a coach. They've been dealing with the obstacles from the past and now there's space to look at their current reality and the future in a different way. The therapy work done by the individual, with the support of a specialist, helps them to claim back full ownership over their life.

I believe coaching happens where the past meets the future. That moment is 'the now', also described as 'the present'. And 'the present' is nothing but a combination of experiences from the past and expectations from the future.

That combination informs us about how we perceive this moment, today. Our coachee does not experience the past, nor the future, as something traumatic and paralysing. They find themselves facing a choice and the coaching empowers them to make these authentic and resonating choices, leading to specific actions. And when their choices and actions work out differently from what they expected, they are able to learn from this and, where needed, adjust their course.

One of my slogans is: "Nobody needs a coach, yet everyone could do with one". Life is constantly happening to all of us, and a coach, as your partner in a creative and thought-provoking process, can help you to keep optimising your potential. And to play with that quote, maybe we could say: "Not everyone could do with a therapist but sometimes you need one?".

To wrap up and summarise, I've made you a very brief overview of some of the (generalised) differences between therapy and coaching.

***

Q26: How to work with rational coachees?

“My coachee is so in her head, everything I tried to connect her to her body, failed!”. Probably a sentence many of us can relate to.

“When I invite my coachee to explore his emotions, he prefers to keep it professional”. Another well-known challenge for coaches.

When this happens, many of us either start to question themselves as a coach or describe their coachee as ‘difficult’.

Another one of my Golden Rules says there are no difficult coachees, instead, they ‘just’ need to learn ‘how to play the game’. They ‘just’ need to learn how to reconnect with being fully human. I know, I know... easier said than done!

One of the first things every human being does, right after being born, is cry. And if you don’t, the doctor will help you with that. With the first cry, we open up our lungs so we can inhale life.

The next thing, if all goes well, is that we’re given to our mother so we can feel her body against ours. Another essential experience for the newborn.

Funny, right, the first two things we do in life is experience emotions and embodiment. Maybe a fun story to share with your coachees? 😉

If we then keep looking at how the process of growing up unfolds, especially before we can speak, it’s all through embodied experiences and emotions. Babies communicate through body language and emotions. Totally normal and acceptable.

Though for many it becomes less and less normal and acceptable whilst growing up. Our parents prepare us for the ‘real world’, bit by bit, and teach us how to ‘behave’. Fewer emotions, less play and less embodiment. The trouble really begins when we go to school and if that doesn’t ‘solve’ it for you, you’re going to find out quickly in your first job. Society often rewards us for acting like human doings rather than human beings. A robot without emotions but full of logic and reason. Again, context for us that could actually be really helpful as context for our coachees.

I give coachees this context and explain why coaches find it important to work with the whole person, and in addition I sometimes give them 'homework' to play and feel. When they have kids, you can ask them to be more conscious about how they use their body when they play with them. And what emotions they experience during that playtime.

When they do sports, ask them to pay attention to how their body is informing them. Or when they feel tired, ask them to take some notes about which part(s) of them is/are tired.

Ask them to go to a museum or into nature and rather than rushing through it, experience their environment. How is it to feel that fresh air in their lungs? How do they feel taking in the beauty they see? Or ask them to go back to that moment they held their child for the first time, to that moment 'it' happened between them and their partner. When they lost a loved one. I'm pretty sure these are all moments full of emotions and physical sensations. Because this is a natural part of being human.

I'm sure you can think of a wide variety of things you can ask your coachee to experiment with to help them reconnect with their body and emotions. Reconnect with being and feeling alive. Meet them where they are. Acknowledge what already is and champion them for what you believe they can become.

Oh, and give yourself permission to role model using your body and expressing emotions. Get up from your chair and move your body. Show them your authentic range. Laugh with them, cry with them, celebrate with them, be angry for the sake of their growth.

Because maybe, what you see in your coachees is just a mirror of your behaviour...?

***

Q27: How to hold emotions in coaching?

Busy, busy, busy. One appointment after the other. Hard stops. Endless to do lists. Not enough hours in the day, days in the week. Is it already almost Christmas again...?!? These feelings are likely rather familiar for many of us, since this is very often the vibe we pick up from our coachees. We are just one of the twenty appointments they have on that day. They arrive slightly late and request to end a few minutes early because... (fill in one of the reasons mentioned above). Too much to do. Not enough time. Let's hurry.

When we check in with the coachee, this is how they come to the call. The space is filled with rush, stress, a fear of running behind even more. We hear it in the way they speak. A certain look in their eyes. When they start the session with you, you hear the notifications from other applications on their computer, trying to get their attention. Their phone rings, they pause in the middle of their sentence, pick up the device and when they see who's calling, a sigh comes out of their mouth. Combined with the expected eye-roll. A small hesitation and they decide it's a call that can't be ignored. "I'm so sorry, I really need to answer this one. Give me a second," and before you can respond, they mute the call with you. You are parked in the 'waiting zone'. Since the video is still on, you can witness the gestures and facial expressions of your coachee. You don't need to hear the words to understand that the call isn't a relaxed one.

The second they asked for becomes a few minutes and when they unmute themselves again, they give you another apology and ask, "Where were we?".

You remind your coachee that the session has started yet it hasn't actually begun yet... "What do you need to put on hold to allow yourself to focus on the 'me-time' in this coaching session?" This is your attempt to get your coachee's attention, with the intention to make something out of this session, but even without noticing it, the pressure has been getting under your skin. "Nothing, I'm fine, let's get started," is how your coachee responds.

You once heard a smart-ass coach saying that 'FINE' stands for 'Feelings I'm Not Expressing' and you play that back to the coachee. Next, you ask them if it is okay to do a conscious check-in using the four ways of knowing. They nod as a sign of permission, even though you can see in their eyes it's not fully clear to them what you mean by this. So, you give context and share the four short sentences, inviting them to complete them.

"My mind is..."
"My heart is..."
"My body is..."
"My spirit is..."

Your coachee pauses for a moment. You see them swallow. When opening their mouth and taking a breath before speaking, all of a sudden they close their mouth again. Another swallow and a quick look to the right, away from the screen. Another attempt to speak.

"My mind is... racing." A pause.

"My heart is..." – and whilst your coachee puts a hand on their heart, they continue with a softer voice... – "my heart is beating fast." Another pause.

You hold the silence.

"My body is... like it's running on empty." The mask drops and no more keeping up appearances. Another quick look away from the screen and their eyes water up.

You hold the silence.

"My spirit is... just so tired," and whilst these words come out of their mouth, their head drops and wants to just rest in their hands.

You hold the silence.

Your coachee looks up at you in the eyes. You both hold the silence.

After another deep sigh, the coachee then asks: "And what should I do about this shitty feeling?". This is the moment where you have a choice, dear colleague. Will you follow your coachee's almost predictable request to move away from their feelings? Or will you choose to slow down and invite your coachee to explore these emotions?

This is the moment where you can expect Saboteurs to whisper, or even scream, in your coachee's ears: "Move on! Don't look into this! Too painful, not good for you! Toughen up, emotions are a sign of weakness!". And so on... At the same time, don't be surprised if it is the coach's Saboteur who will try to convince them not to go there: "You are not strong enough to hold the space for your coachee. This will remind you of your own emotions, get out of here!". And so on...

Frequently, the coach decides to jump to the 'solution'. Well, it is assumed to be a solution yet in reality we miss a chance to grow by setting a stuck emotion, an unused energy, free. Jumping to the other side of the pool is not doing your coachee a favour and only pleasing your and their Saboteur. Nothing will change when we do that!

It takes courage for both the coach and the coachee to consciously face these emotions. Slowing down and not running away from our feelings needs to become the new norm. As children we were a lot better equipped to be fully in our emotions and simply experience them. Allow them to inform us about what was going on inside of us. We knew what it was to be fully alive, with the highs and the lows. When joyful, we laughed until it hurt our bellies or until we lost our breath. When angry, we made fists with our hands and shouted it out. When sad, we cried, sobbed even. Until there were no more tears to cry. We – were – fully – alive!

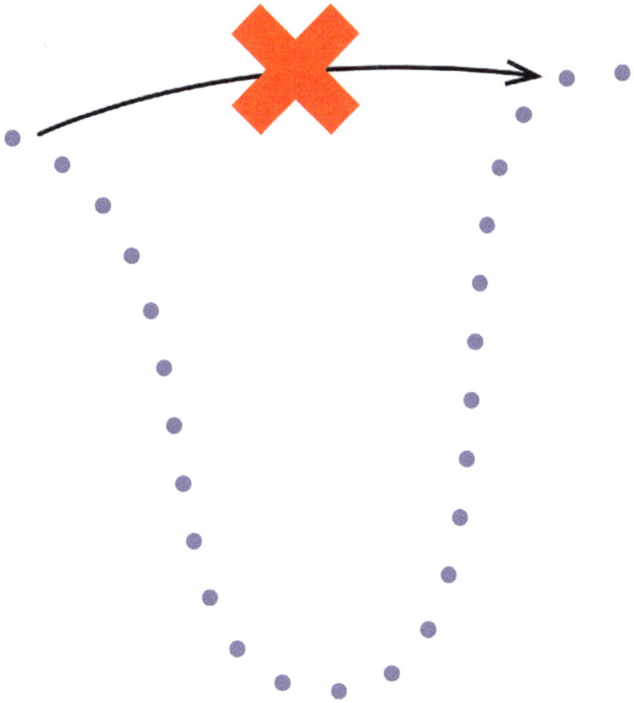

Then we went to school and the world started to tell us how to behave. We graduated in keeping up appearances. We found a job and became the role we were hired for, and in most cases, expressing your emotions was not part of the job description. We were transformed from human beings into human doings, the new level of sophistication. When we had moments where we were reminded of being human after all, we quickly moved on. Toughened up. Swallowed our feelings away and with that, put up a mask. A mask with FINE written all over it: Feelings I'm Not Expressing.

Many of our coachees come to coaching programmed in this way. So when we ask them what's going on, they have simply been trained to ignore that question, put on the mask and quickly move on. When the coach is courageous enough to call that out and invite them to slow down and take a closer look at whatever is going on, we do them a huge favour. We offer them a way back to being alive, to being human. Slowing down is the only way to move forward with this. Although it may feel counterintuitive, slowing down is actually the quickest route to rediscovering what it means to be fully human and alive.

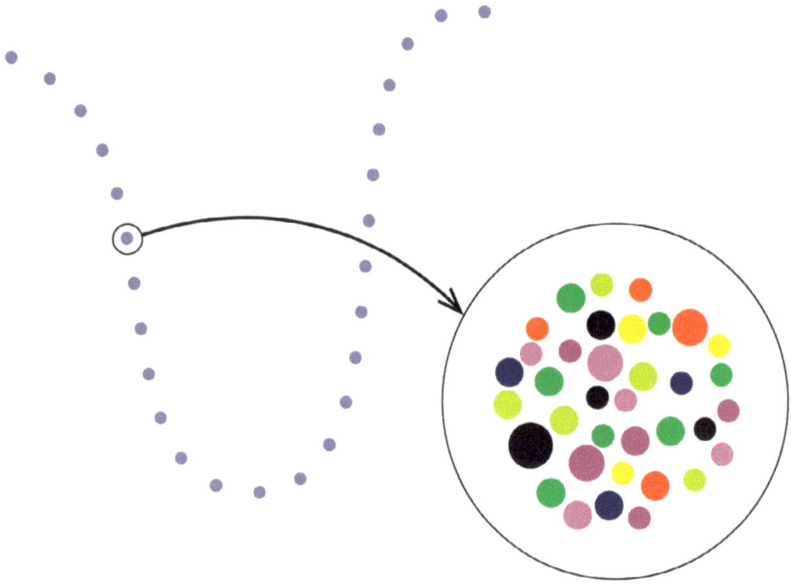

The curve in this image is often used to describe the process our coachees go through when exploring locked away emotions. Though there is no rule about how much time this should take, the tendency from both coach and coachee is to go too fast. We need to invite our coachees to slow down enough to actually explore each and every moment as a precious opportunity for new discovery. Coaches like to talk about 'the now'. 'Now' is this very moment, that part of life we're experiencing in this second. Every dot in this curve is such a 'now'. Every dot is worth being explored and taken a closer look at. When examined closely, as if under a microscope, this dot could reveal a hidden treasure that's waiting for our coachee to be reclaimed. What at first sight may look like any other dot, when we really slow down and zoom in, can turn out to be a colourful place, one that could open our coachee's eyes, their heart, their whole being to the essence of life that wants to be lived. Fully.

***

Q28: How can we keep perspective exercises from becoming dull?

Without trying to be funny, this question holds a perspective. It is a perspective, and maybe even an assumption, that perspective work gets boring for our coachees.

I get this question frequently during the Co-Active Certification programme when we're taking a deep dive into the Balance Principle. And the question is often asked during the Balance course of the Intermediate programme as well, so it's clearly something people are curious about. It might be just a perspective, but every perspective holds at least some truth.

Balance is one of the three Principles in the Co-Active model: Fulfillment, Balance and Process (more on these in question 57). Based on the relationship the coachee has with the topic they bring to the session, the coach chooses one of them to start the exploration phase. The chosen principle may evolve during the session, or the session may combine multiple principles.

The coach will choose Balance when the coachee feels stuck about how to look at a certain topic, person or situation. We generally choose this principle when the coachee speaks in 'absolutes': "I tried everything, but nothing works", or "It's always been like this and it'll never change". Another popular one: "This is just how we always do it here and it won't change".

The coach starts out by helping the coachee to make a distinction between the actual topic and the way they look at this topic. Here it is important to make the topic really neutral (making it a noun is often very helpful) because adjectives usually hold some charge, a perspective. From there we help the coachee to explore multiple, randomly (!) chosen other perspectives. Just like a different pair of glasses through which the coachee looks at the same topic.

After looking into three or four perspectives, they are quickly being revisited and, maybe with the help of the Leader Within, the coachee will choose a perspective that resonates most for them.

After that, we start a fun and creative brainstorming activity that looks like the coach and the coachee are playing tennis, each time throwing in something new. A way to be, coming from this new perspective, or something they could do. The coach is actively engaged here and throws in fun and unexpected things. Brainstorming is out of the box thinking after all, right?

The big list from the brainstorm will be reduced by the coachee to a few things they feel like committing to. Next to saying this out loud, some kind of ritual will deepen the coachee's relationship with what they say 'yes' or 'no' to. The coach can really tap into their creativity when setting up this ritual.

With the commitment frequently being something rather open or abstract, it needs to be translated into a specific action, where the coachee also chooses what kind of accountability would serve them.

The above may feel like a short lecture about the principle of Balance – ah well, maybe it is – but I hope you've noticed some of the keywords are creativity, random, play, and out of the box.

Though the steps in Balance may feel somewhat formulaic, when the coach allows themselves to fully tap into their range and playfulness, this will never get boring.

Also, you as a coach may have done this many times, but for your individual coachee, it may only be the second or third time.

Additionally, so far I've been describing all the steps in the 'official order'. Don't let that confuse you! Yes, you can do it in this order and I'm sure it'll serve your coachee. But why not choose a part of it and only do that with your coachee? When you dare to 'dance', when you dare to play, when you are willing to bring your full authentic range to your coaching, your coachee will never get bored!

So, dear colleague, when you feel your Balance coaching might get dull and boring, explore where you can tap into your range more, in order to 'unbore' the Co-Active Principle of Balance.

***

Q29: How do you approach coaching for high-pressure situations, such as leadership during a crisis?

Great question! And this is exactly what some of our coachees experience, maybe even on a daily basis.

There is a fair chance that, due to the high pressure, they also feel they have very little time for things, let alone some time for themselves. Intellectually they understand it's good to do so, yet they feel their reality simply doesn't give them the space for it. There's always something or someone claiming their time. Even when they do schedule sessions, don't be surprised to see them cancelled or they simply don't show up. The fire they needed to deal with was more important...

The first thing that comes up is to create a Designed Alliance that's very specific for the situation of this coachee. Where it's, of course, essential the coach does not forget their own needs and limits! No matter how 'important' the coachee may be, a coaching relationship needs to be based on equal partnership.

The fact that the coach models their limits and needs, can actually be an eye-opener for the coachee: "You mean, saying no is an option? It's okay to claim something for yourself?".

During the actual coaching, I've learned that 'holding the space' for them is already a huge gift. The time you have with them, is probably one of the exceptional moments where they do not have to be on full alert, ready for the next fire to deal with.

Giving them space to 'clear', to vent all the pressure they've been building up, can give them back the capacity to breathe.

Maybe this is 'all' you do in the first few sessions and this is the buildup towards them really starting to trust this unique kind of relationship. What I often do during these first sessions, is 'discovery work on the go'. You pick up a value here and there. You hear more about what triggers them. What they find important in their role as a leader and what kind of impact they like to have. And how reality is perhaps vastly different from what they hope for.

You get to know them better and better, also by asking about their private life. Their family, hobbies, sports, what they like to do in their free time. Maybe they have some heroes in their life or from movies, books or history. There's a fair chance they'll also share parts of their life story, their highs and lows in life.

All the information you collect that way is contributing to their 'Manual of Self' (see question 48). You can create a list of values, input for their vision for their life, their personal heroes, and bit by bit you start to see a profile of the unique person you're working with.

With a growing trust in the relationship, they feel safe to start using coaching for what, at the end of the day, it is meant to be. Working on specific topics, usually to work towards some bigger goals.

Bottom line is:

- Design the relationship very consciously.
- Invest time to win their trust.
- Be creative in how to do discovery work.
- When you feel the relationship is ready for it, exploring actual topics.

***

Q30: How to work with Limiting Beliefs?

When people experience dissonance, they're not living in line with their most authentic and empowered self. They're not living in line with their 'Big Why' or their personal values. Sometimes it's not very clear to them what is off, but they for sure feel something isn't okay for them.

This situation, of experiencing 'something's off', can become the topic they bring to a session.

While working on this, they start to move towards a change, which is the wake-up call for their Saboteurs.

Saboteurs are allergic to change and they'll do everything they can to avoid this from happening. So far, most likely nothing new for you.

I'm giving you this intro to underline there are two forms of 'resistance' against change. One is the Saboteur, the other is 'Limiting Beliefs'.

Limiting Beliefs are like stuck perspectives on steroids, old stories that are not, or no longer, serving the coachee yet they hold on to them. One day, something happened or someone said something to them which was the starting point for a story that, over time, got completely blown out of proportion.

Very quick example: as a kid at some point my father told me, after I'd been helping someone with odd jobs for a full day, that I wasn't supposed to ask for money. That very short sentence kept echoing in my head and over time my relationship with money became impacted by it. When I started my own business, that of course wasn't very helpful... This limiting belief was something I brought to my coach and after working on this for some time, things shifted.

When we're working on Saboteurs and Limiting Beliefs, we need to make a distinction between the two. To simplify things:

- Saboteurs: maintaining the status quo by hindering change

- Limiting Beliefs: old, unsupportive stories based on a past experience yet defining the coachee's view on something in the present.
- To support the coachee to work with their Limiting Beliefs, personally I find it helpful to ask the coachee to:
- Write down, preferably by hand, the old story in detail.
- Read your own story and highlight each part that's not serving you (any more)
- Reflect on which values are not honoured because of the story, and how
- Start writing a new story, fully in line with your values, an expression of your Big Why (again, preferably handwritten)
- Read this story a few times and keep finetuning it (reading it out loud can be helpful)
- Optional: a ritual to say goodbye to the old story, for instance by burning the paper on which it's written
- Optional: creating an Ally (an imaginary internal friend) who can support you sticking to and expressing the new story
- Optional: creating a structure, a physical reminder, for the new story. This is also where embodiment can be very helpful, like how do you stand or speak when you come from this new story.
- After working on and integrating the new story in between sessions, the coachee often finds it helpful to share the new story with their coach by reading it out loud. The job of the coach is to witness the new story and to acknowledge and champion the storyteller.

From there the coach supports the coachee to further integrate the new story in their daily life, for instance by creating specific actions based on the new story.

The accountability around these actions will further help the coachee to deepen their learning around all these new possibilities.

***

Q31: Why is using the body important in coaching?

We human beings learn in many different ways. We are wonderfully complex, multilayered, with a rich variety in how we collect, process, store, and utilise information.

I'm convinced we only know parts about the richness and diversity of the resources we have as human beings.

As coaches, we often speak about the four ways of knowing: mind, heart, body and spirit.

Many human beings are most familiar with the mind as a resource for our wisdom. And René Descartes famously stated: "Cogito, ergo sum". For those less familiar with Latin: "I think, therefore I am".

Our mind, our brain, is a very impressive, smart and creative 'supercomputer'. So clearly not a resource to be underestimated! Thinking is great, don't you think 😉

Our heart is so much more than the big muscle pumping blood through our body. It's also often referred to when we speak about love. The heart seems to be widely accepted as the place where love lives. But that's not all! The heart is also storing experiences and creating wisdom from there. Instead of AI, HI: Heart Intelligence.

Without going into more details about the heart as a resource for wisdom, I do want to point at something we've probably all said or heard several times in our life. And that is, when we ask people for advice, the encouraging answer is: "Just follow your heart". Why would we collectively say that, if we don't somehow know there's truth in it...?

Before looking at the body, let's talk about the spirit. Others call it intuition or gut feeling. Whatever way you describe it, it's another rich resource where we can tap into the wisdom above and beyond logic and reason. We've all experienced situations when there was no logical reason why we should look over our shoulder and notice that friend we otherwise would have missed. Or when clear information was missing, but we still knew whether to turn left or right; literally or metaphorically, we felt which direction to take. At C-Suite level, major decisions are being made where the main data is someone's intuition. Because we just feel that's the way to move forward.

It may take our coachee some time, they might need some additional context, but more often than not, they join us in tapping into these three resources. Why would it be different when it's about the body?

We can explain why the other three 'ways of knowing' are really cool resources, so what makes it so hard for some of us to use the body in a similar way?

Here's a thought, let me just try something: everybody has Limiting Beliefs, stuck perspectives on steroids by which we design certain parts of our life. 'Everybody' includes us as coaches. So maybe it's the coach's perspective on embodiment, that becomes the hindering factor?

I'm going to ask you a few questions, so you can check if this may be applicable to you:

- How much of your coaching do you do from your chair only?
- When you get up, is there something actually changing in your coaching or does it (quickly) continue as if you were sitting?
- When you ask the famous question "Where do you feel this in your body?", how do you support your coachee to not just answer from their mind, but to take some time to check in with their physical sensations?
- How often do you invite your coachee for a guided visualisation to do a body scan?
- When you invite your coachee to embody something, how much of that do you do with them, for instance through mirroring?

When the answer to the questions above is 'just sometimes or even 'never', maybe that holds an invitation to further self-exploration for you? And sometimes you can do all of the above with lots of enthusiasm, and still your coachee is hesitant to play along. Maybe you did find that 'unwilling or difficult' coachee? Don't think so! You may have a coachee that's so used to primarily tapping into the wisdom from their wonderful mind, they lost some of the connection with other parts of self. Let's start with meeting them where they are and not make them feel bad for any of it. Before they're willing, or able, to get curious about how their body is constantly communicating with them, they might first need to understand how that works and why it's supportive to our learning process. Have a conversation about it with them, give examples. Very simple, like "How are we informed we're hungry or cold?". They'll know the answer to that!

Or how amazing it is when our hand pulls back when we're about to burn our fingers, which happens even quicker than our brains can process the potential danger. Your hand isn't going to wait for that! 😉

As babies, we were informing and teaching the rest of the system through various physical experiences and experiments that stimulate neural connections and cognitive development. The body first, the brain follows. For example, when a baby touches different textures (soft, rough, smooth), they do not only experience physical sensations but also form connections in the brain that support tactile perception. Or when they are repeating movements like kicking or waving arms which creates and strengthens neural pathways. This repetition is crucial for learning motor patterns and memory, helping babies develop muscle memory and coordination.

Several more examples could be given, but you get the picture: we (also) teach our whole self through embodied experiences. Our coachees will usually be adults, but they still learn in the same way.

Just as we as coaches 'focus on the whole person' when we work with our coachee to listen to them on Levels 2 and 3, we also encourage them to use their whole self in service to their own exploration and growth.

***

Q32: What advice would you give to someone just starting their journey as a coach?

Though giving advice is 'against the rules' of what coaches do, I sometimes 'sin' against the rules so this time going to give it 😉

Refraining from giving advice is probably one of the most common challenges for beginning coaches. I've never met a coach whose previous experience did not have some component of advice giving and because you were trained and gained experience, you became the specialist in a specific field. People worked with you exactly for that reason; they wanted you to advise them from your expertise. And you were rewarded and respected for this. Rightfully! Because when hired as the expert, be the expert.

But giving advice is not part of coaching, since in coaching, the coachee is seen as the expert, so our need to give advice needs to be self-managed by us as coaches.

Here's a tip: write three different job descriptions for yourself: one for you as a coach, one for a private role and another one for a professional role. For each one, think of five core competencies specific to that role. When you're about to start a coaching session, look at them and consciously choose one competency for this session.

Another common question from new coaches is around niching. To niche or not to niche, that's the question! Many new coaches start looking for coachees in their former work environment. That's easy, since that's where they know a lot of people. The problem is that they also know you and often see you as the expert they've worked with. Guess why it's so hard to coach and not consult...?

In the beginning of your coaching career, it's best to work with a wide variety of people so you expand your range and learn how to do your magic in all sorts of environments. My perspective, especially in the early days, is that a niche is often confused with an easy way to find coachees in your previous field of expertise. This often leads to confused coachees because they don't get your new way of helping them. And a frustrated coach because you're in a constant battle between roles.

Tip: Don't look for a niche and if, with time, it wants to happen, trust it'll find you. Additionally, I would advise you to make your niche a certain type of person, not a specific topic.

Another tip: prepare yourself for a work environment where you'll be, and feel, alone a lot! After saying goodbye to your coachee, there's just no one to talk to. Constantly in service to others yet nobody there for you... It's essential to surround yourself with like-minded colleagues with whom you can share stories and support and inspire each other. Avoid becoming the 'lonely coach'.

Tip: Join an inspiring and supportive coaching community.

***

Q33: How is coaching connected to spirituality?

Let's start with asking ourselves what spirituality actually is? In previous questions we looked at what coaching is, so let's put coaching and spirituality next to each other. For some people, 'spirituality' is the same as religion. My perspective is that they are actually two different things. While doing some additional research on this, I bumped into this explanation: *"Religion is a specific set of organised beliefs and practices, usually shared by a community or group. Spirituality is more of an individual practice and has to do with having a sense of peace and purpose. It also relates to the process of developing beliefs around the meaning of life and connection with others."*

If we look for a link to coaching, the keywords in this description of spirituality are: individual practice, a sense of peace and purpose, meaning of life and connection with others.

When we look at what we work on with our coachees, this is very similar. The word spirituality holds the word 'spirit', and one of the ways to describe that word is 'essence', who we are at our core. Coaches work with the essence of a human being. Who are you? Who do you want to become? What really matters to you? What's the essence of your existence?

Walking with my dogs isn't therapy, but it can be very therapeutic. Coaching isn't spirituality, but it can be very spiritual. We support people to connect with, explore and create from their essence, their spirit and their core.

***

Q34: Can coaching skills benefit our personal lives?

Oh yeah! I actually think this is the reason why coaching found me. I didn't become a coach because I am so smart or talented. Nor because I know how to solve all the problems in the world. I am convinced that coaching found me because I still had to learn so much about how to show up in life; yes, just day to day life.

From a 'judgement machine on two legs', I needed to learn how to be genuinely curious. From being very fast with my answers and so called 'brilliant solutions', I needed to learn how to listen. Like, really listen. Not just to the words, but to everything that is being communicated.

From asking questions in order to figure out solutions or receive confirmation for my ideas and opinions, I needed to start asking questions that would take the other person on a little journey of exploration. Looking for their way forward, rather than mine.

From being primarily driven by what my wonderful brain had to offer, I needed to learn to include my other resources of wisdom.

From telling others what to do and how to do it, I had to make the shift to asking others how they wanted to move forward. From an instructor to a guide, accompanying the other person on their journey of growth. And I can add 'a few' more things to the list of why coaching had to find me and teach me so many valuable lessons.

I am a huge fan of the Co-Active model. For a long time, it was called the Co-Active Coaching model. With time we learned this model is not only a great model for coaching, it is also super helpful as a communication model, a model for how we human beings can be with each other.

As tempting as it may seem, I am not inviting you to start coaching everyone you meet, as a spontaneous act of kindness. Being in a coaching relationship requires a conscious choice from both parties and a clear design. But for listening in a different way, asking a different kind of questions, just to give a few examples, we do not need anyone's permission. Actually, I am sure that being with each other in a more conscious way, inspired by some coaching skills and ways of being, will make the world a more peaceful and inclusive place.

My dream is for children to learn some of these skills from primary school onwards, so it becomes the new normal for how we interact with each other.

***

Q35: Are coaching skills useful as management skills?

Another, 'Oh Yes'! Coaching skills are really helpful in day-to-day life, but I am also super excited about the positive impact coaching can have on supporting managers in their roles.

'Manage' comes from the Latin word 'manus', which means 'hand'. In that sense, managing something originally meant to, in some way, control it with your hands. Managing people became 'putting them in your hands', so the manager could control how things happened. That they were done in the way the manager wanted it and planned it.

Over time, we came to realise that managing processes requires a different set of skills than 'controlling' people. Indeed, we learned that human beings flourish more when they are inspired to use their talents in the best possible way so they can contribute to the goals of the team. Many say that with that shift in how to look at people, managers evolved into leaders who treat their team members in a very different way. And this is exactly where coaching skills come in. The word 'leadership' finds its origin in the Old English word 'lithan' which literally means 'to go' and also 'to guide'. A leader guides people to where they want to go, rather than tells them what to do. Building on this, a manager who leads people asks them where they want to go. What drives them, what makes them get out of bed in the morning. When a manager becomes a leader who guides the people they've been given to lead, they become curious. Therefore, they ask different kinds of questions. They listen to connect rather than to analyse and criticise.

Yes, I understand that there are situations where there's no or little space to practise all of the above. Sometimes stuff just needs to get done, quick action is needed and orders may have to be followed. Yet this is only sustainable when before and after such moments, the communication and interaction are different. My wife is a volunteer fire fighter. Her commanding officer would never ask her how she feels when responding to a fire. What motivates her to put her life at risk. And you can think of many more coach-like questions that would be but just plain stupid to ask at such a moment. Orders need to be followed, things must be done. She is willing to put her safety, her life even, in the hands of her colleagues and commanding officer, because they have worked hard, spent lots of time building a relationship where they can blindly trust each other. Where they know from each other who they are and what drives them. And after such big events, they invest time to evaluate, to learn, to reconnect and to explore not only what they could do differently the next time, but also how they want to be with each other. There's a fair chance her commanding officer has had lots of training: he not only knows what he is doing, but he also knows how to show up as a leader and inspire his team. And that includes lots of coaching skills.

Effective managers have become leaders of people, using coaching skills to motivate people and bring out the best in them.

***

Q36: Imposter, imposter, how do we deal with you?

There were several questions around this topic. How to support coachees who are hijacked by this 'paralysing energy', and how to deal with it as a coach? For instance, when they start questioning if they've got what it takes, not only to coach but also to make it a sustainable business. Funny right, we coaches, we deal with the same challenges as our coachees...

When we speak about this, it's often referred to as 'Imposter Syndrome'. A syndrome is not a disease (nor a disorder). A little bit of research on this topic leads to the following information: *"The basic difference between the two terms relates to the symptoms that they produce. A disease can be defined as a health condition that has a clearly defined reason behind it. A syndrome (from the Greek word meaning 'run together'), however, may produce a number of symptoms without an identifiable cause. A syndrome refers to a group of symptoms, while a disease refers to an established condition.*

The symptom caused by a syndrome does not have an established reason behind it. In case of a disease, the cause is identified. Treatment of a syndrome is mainly symptomatic. In case of a disease, the underlying cause is treated. A disease causes changes in the anatomy; a syndrome may not produce any such changes".

People who struggle with imposter syndrome believe that they are undeserving of their achievements and the high esteem in which they are, in fact, generally held. They feel that they aren't as competent or intelligent as others might think—and that soon enough, people will discover the truth about them. Those with imposter syndrome—which is not an official diagnosis—they are often well accomplished; they may hold high office or have numerous academic degrees.

It happens to many of us. Around 25 to 30 percent of high achievers are likely to suffer from imposter syndrome. And around 70 percent of adults may experience imposter syndrome to a certain extent at least once in their lifetime, research suggests.

Overcoming imposter syndrome involves changing a person's mindset about their own abilities. Imposters often feel like they don't belong, so acknowledging their expertise and accomplishments is key, as is reminding them that they earned their place in their academic or professional environment.

As coaches we can invite our coachees to stay focused on measuring their own achievements, instead of comparing themselves to others. Similar to perfectionists, people with imposter syndrome often put a lot of pressure on themselves to complete every task flawlessly; they fear that any mistake will reveal to others that they aren't good or smart enough for the job. And by the way, coaches potentially experience the same as their coachees.

A way to help coachees stay focused is to request them to journal and question their own thoughts. When a thought is not supportive, not acknowledging who they really are or downplaying what they accomplished, we can ask them to rewrite it into the actual truth. That is probably easier said than done. This is a process that often requires repetition, and it may take months. Additionally, self-affirmations are supportive ways to reprogram the thinking of our coachees, as well as conversations with someone they trust, someone who loves and supports them. Receiving their Acknowledgements and Championing are such a blessing.

In the coaching, you can work on normalising 'failed first attempts'. After all, FAIL is an acronym for First Attempt In Learning. Consciously choose activities where they know they need to learn by doing. Doing new things always includes failed attempts, and this can help the coachee embrace mistakes, not succeeding a first time, as a normality.

Another exercise is the art of making distinctions. We might fail, but that doesn't make us a failure. We might lose, but that doesn't make us a loser. Others might be better at what we do, but that doesn't make us or what we do worthless.

Finally, it can be very supportive for the coachee to gain some knowledge around the Imposter Syndrome. Part of the suffering people experience is due to a lack of understanding about what is going on, which often leads to blowing things out of proportion.

Coaches and their coachees have one thing in common: they are both human and experience the same kind of challenges in life. Therefore, the same kind of work needs to be done by both.

***

Q37: What are creative ways to work with Leader Within & Allies?

This is a beautiful tool in Co-Active coaching to support coachees to explore and connect with a specific part of their inner resources, a tool to give a voice to the multiple versions of 'self' we all have. I know many Co-Active coaches love this. And many struggle with it. Oops!

One of the reasons why some colleagues struggle with Leader Within, is probably because they lack context. This tool is one of the examples where the profession of coaching borrowed something from therapy: Voice Dialogue. Though some resources tell us this started about 100 years ago, many see Dr. Hal Stone and Dr. Sidra Stone as the pioneers of Voice Dialogue. They started working with it in the 70s. The bottom line of Voice Dialogue is that we all have multiple selves, and they all have a voice. Other terminology used here is 'inner selves', 'parts', 'sub-personalities' and 'energy patterns', as well as archetypes. Voice Dialogue gives us the ability to handle, or manage, our 'selves' in a more conscious way. There is a lot of (neuro)science behind this and many colleagues and neighbouring professions even specialise in this important tool to bring people in touch with their true self/selves.

We all have the ability to have a good conversation with ourselves. It's even ingrained in the language we use, for instance when we say "Part of me says this, but another part of me says that". Or we joke about "Me, myself and I". We now know this isn't a joke, but a proven part of us. Remember this, when you invite people for a party, you might get three times as many guests as you expected. 😉

I am sharing the above because many coaches aren't aware that the origin of this tool is to be found in therapy, and, as mentioned, the theory is based on neuroscience research. It's not only the coach who sometimes needs to understand what the origin of a tool is before they can embrace it. The same goes for our coachees. Some people really need some context before they are willing to experiment with a new tool.

One of the ways to support our coachees to get in touch with these Inner Resources, is through visualisation. Some love it and can't get enough of it. Amazing! And some look at you like "Seriously... Am I paying for this!?".

This means we need multiple ways to approach this concept! I believe it is important that we get to know the context of our coachee's life so we use metaphors that work for them. When we work with a plumber, their work, their language, their tools, their metaphors are rather different from when we work with an IT specialist. We connect with our coachee by using examples, metaphors and language from their world.

Example: You coach a CEO. You suggest an exercise where you're going to hire a management team to run the organisation called 'Their Life'. So you start by asking what the three or four core competencies are for the CEO they trust so much so that they want to hire them. A smart CEO hires a few specialists around their boardroom table like Alexander the Great, the 'Strategist' or Christina the 'Banker'. And possibly also some creative and/or critical voices. Like Aladdin the 'Rebel' or Bobby the 'five-year old'. Or Serena, the 'Tattoo

Artist'. They give very unexpected and out of the box perspectives. For each member you ask your coachee to give some core competencies and within 15 minutes you do not only have their CEO (Leader Within) but also the other boardroom members (Allies). You could give them some homework to maybe create an image, or any other creative representation of their team, and encourage them to start having conversations with them. To consult their advisors.

Finally, a very short alternative approach. Ask your coachee to imagine that their best friend joins the conversation. This person has known you for years, loves you, is straightforward and kickass when needed. Then ask: "What would this friend say?".

***

Q38: How to support our coachee to stay committed?

Coaching is hard work for the coachee. Sometimes the results come quickly, usually it takes longer. In general, we could say real change takes time, because the coachee needs space to try things, experiment, succeed, fail, learn, try again, and gradually grow into new patterns.

Many of us like to see results quickly, preferably with not too much effort. We like it easy, don't we 😉 And if it gets tough, we might get disappointed, with a fair chance of giving up. I say 'we', because isn't this how it works for most of us?

Our coachees come to coaching with some specific goals they want to work towards. There's a fair chance the coach designs a package of multiple sessions with them, spread out over several months. We know things take time and explain this to our coachee. They are eager to start the process and accept 'the deal'. But maybe they are not fully understanding what they say 'yes' to, from a time perspective. They may even wonder why the coach opts for a longer process than only two, maybe three sessions. But hey, the coach has experience so let's go for it!

After a couple of sessions, the coachee finds it harder and harder to remain patient and wait for the results. The motivation is dropping and the coach may even sense some resistance. At that point, the coach might feel pressure to keep the coachee going. It's not the coach's job to start working harder. One of my Golden Rules for Coaching is that the coach is responsible for the process, the coachee for the content. Part of the coach's responsibility is to hold a meta view over the process and normalise the ups and downs in the way the coachee is able to show up. After all, they are not unwilling, it just gets harder. So what to do?

I'd start by simply articulating what you observe and sharing this with the coachee. It's important to do this without any form of judgement, so it might be smart to give some context regarding why you're sharing your observation. Remember, the coachee is often new to the game and we need to explain to them how the game might unfold.

After a few sessions, there's a fair chance that some change is already happening and, as we know, this is the wake-up call for Saboteurs. To avoid more change from happening, it's a rather strategic move from the Saboteur to steal the motivation from the coachee away. That way the coachee might give up, thus no more change. Victory for the Saboteur!

Simply explaining this to the coachee and helping them see what's happening, is sometimes sufficient.

Coming from the bigger picture, the coach could also show this to the coachee. Verbalise the journey they've already travelled and the steps they've made towards their goals. Acknowledge them for how they have been showing up and champion them for what you see is about to come. These two skills make our coachee really feel seen and it gives them 'air under their wings' and will support them to keep going, even when the going gets tough.

Additionally, it's important to keep the coachee connected to the goals they came to coaching for. What was it again that made them choose to make this investment, in time, energy and money? Maybe in the meantime you've been working on values. Which values will be lived out more when these goals become a reality? Or, how is achieving these goals an expression of their Big Why, aka Life Purpose? What does their Leader Within, their most empowered self, have to say about the journey they're on?

In essence, we can say that when the dissonance is trying to take over, you should reconnect them with the resonance that drives them.

***

Q39: No topic? Not even a wish! Now what?

Coaching is about exploration, not about explanation. This is the first Golden Rule in my book and I'm using this over and over again to explain an essential part of why coaching exists. We are partnering with our coachees to explore new terrain and not for them to explain to us what they already know. By applying this Golden Rule, we aim to explain why we may intrude when they lose themselves in sharing endless details, when they tell us stories that contribute nothing new, or when they talk about circumstances or other people involved. Of course, they do this with the best intentions because they think we need to know all this context. That we need this context so we can understand what they talk about, maybe sympathise with them, partnering in feeling sorry for them. 'Understanding' is not a coaching skill, but something we do need to understand is that we're not doing our coachees a favour when we do not intrude and allow them to go on and on with their stories!

Part of the job of a coach is to train our coachee on how to be an effective coachee, how to get the most out of their coaching adventure. This includes giving them context on what the purpose of intruding is. Another one is to support them in how to come to a session prepared. Personally, I share a few questions with my coachees that they can use to collect their insights and reflect on the action they agreed to take right after the coaching session, to journal about how things have evolved in the time between the sessions and, last but not least, to prepare for the next session. It is a waste of precious coaching time, after all, to speak in length about things they could have simply captured in an email that the coach could have read prior to the session. This way, the coach too can prepare and connect with what's going on for the coachee. Additionally, journalling is a proven way to get a deeper understanding of what's going on for us, or as coaches like to say, to deepen the learning.

It probably takes a bit of time to get there, yet at some point the coachee understands how to play the game and all goes very smoothly. The coaching gets into a real flow and the sessions are well used. Well done, you two!

And then... 'The Moment'. Your coachee, with an almost 'guilty' expression on their face, shares that they could not think of a topic for today since all is well. The important goals they came to coaching for have been achieved, no new problems came up. All is AMAZING!

At this point, the coach can choose from a variety of approaches to handle the situation. There are several good ways and some not so good ones. Not so good is to invite your Saboteurs and start wondering if you can still be of added value for your coachee from this point onwards. Another not so good one is to rub in your coachee's feeling of guilt and remind them of the agreement that they should always 'come prepared'. Since I know none of these two are options you would choose, let me share one of the supportive options you have.

After acknowledging your coachee for their commitment to keep working on their goals, and actually achieving them, you can invite them to take a look at the bigger picture. "Which bigger picture?", your coachee might ask. Well, there is a lot to be learned about how they have travelled on the journey to get to this wonderful 'peak experience'. We can take a closer look at what they have done to get there. There must have been obstacles on the road whilst they were climbing this mountain. What have they done to deal with them? And how have they been to conquer these obstacles?

Additionally, you can take a closer look at how far they actually are with achieving their goals. Are they indeed achieved or is their Saboteur trying to tell them that 'half done' is enough and that they should not look for more?

The key is to foster learning by reflecting on the journey they've taken.

Let's assume they did indeed fully achieve their goals and that you, of course, not did forget to acknowledge them for how they have been. We can't be generous enough with this after all. The next step is to invite them to look around from where they find themselves at this point in time. I hope the coachee has a big smile on their face when they take in the wonderful view. You are standing next to them and are happy with, and for, them. Then you ask, "What is the impact you want to have from this place?" The coachee looks at you, wondering what you mean by this.

"Well, dear coachee, there is no such thing as not having an impact. From this wonderful place, what is the impact you want to have on the world around you? You are way too generous to just keep it all to yourself. You have a purpose to express. From where you are now, with the stars perfectly lined up for you, what do you want to create? How do you want to show up in the world?"

This is the moment to slow down with your coachee and look at their values and their Big Why, aka Purpose, in life. They are in flow, so you should encourage them to ride this wave consciously. Invite them to look around, to the world around them. Then in the mirror of their own circumstances. From what you have available at this moment, what do you want to create? Additionally, it's wise to have a conversation about how they need to be in order to maintain this moment of flow and fulfillment. It is so precious; it must be safeguarded. Saboteurs will come, circumstances will change, people will mess with you. How to be alert, so you're not taken down by all this?

There is more to be explored though! After consciously taking the time to look at how they got here and what they want to create from this cool place, let's take the time to look at what more life has in store. Let's assume your coachee doesn't want to 'retire from living life to the fullest'. In that case, "What's next?" is a very valid question. After enjoying the view from here for a while, after taking in all the lessons and gifts, new pages of your coachee's 'book of life' want to be written. Do some visioning work with your coachee to explore with them what's around the corner. NO! This is not about always wanting more and bigger! Yet evolution is an unstoppable process so at some point your coachee will be ready for their 'next' thing. Stay curious, because there is always more to explore.

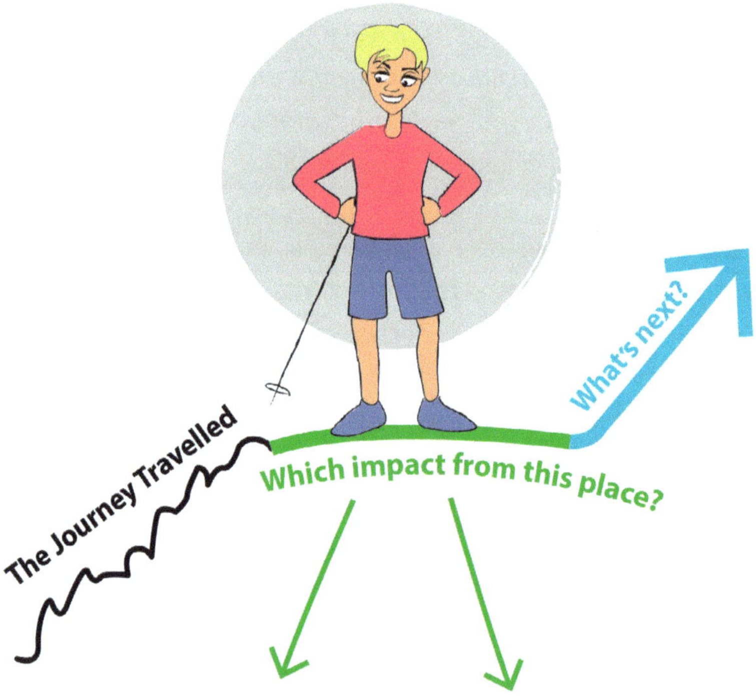

***

Q40: With more experience, does it get easier?

I love what I do. I do what I love. One of the things I love doing is teaching coaching. Like, LOVE doing that!

Almost two decades ago, I got introduced to the Co-Active Model by my teachers – I am still grateful to them, and I fell for it on the spot. It intrigued me from the beginning, though I must admit I didn't fully understand everything it was trying to convey. It was likely more about the vibe I sensed than a clear grasp of what each part of the model meant.

Bit by bit, I tried to get my head around each part of the model and how they related to one another.

Another 'confession': at first, I thought it was entirely about the coachee. When I simply 'implemented the model' I could help the coachee... Okay, you can probably predict how that worked out...

Somewhere during the Co-Active Certification programme, I started to understand that the Co-Active Model was as much about me as it was about the coachee. I started to understand that it wasn't only about the transformation of the coachee. Parts of me also needed to transform in order to show up in line with the essence of the model.

To give just one example, I needed to shift from being overly judgemental to embracing a state of living, breathing curiosity. For this, I needed to embrace other contexts as my new 'come from' as well. An intense and interesting personal development journey began. On that journey, I moved from being just the student, to the student who is also a teacher. Let me explain: over time, I've learned to understand that the most effective way to learn about a certain topic is to teach it.

From here, I'd like to jump ahead to one of the recent courses I've been leading. We were discussing parts of the Co-Active Model and one of the participants shared a thought, which felt more like an assumption. This student stated that it must become a lot easier, with time, to always come from the model and that certain parts would probably hardly need attention any more. That's when I realised that there is no such thing as a Co-Active Model for beginners and a separate one for advanced coaches! A 'Newbie' or a 'Golden Oldie' – they are both still human beings, and they need to be equally aware of the challenges we experience whilst coaching.

The more experienced coach might have an even bigger risk of 'falling from the model' because of the 'arrogance of experience'...

There is no Co-Active Model for experienced coaches, like something you can grow into. No! Well, actually, maybe there is. Take a closer look at it and maybe, dear experienced colleague, you'll discover there are exclamation marks behind certain parts of the model. The sections of the model where our overconfidence in our experience may have caused us to overlook some details.

So, to answer the question if it gets easier with more experience: yes, we may feel more confident and less in doubt about what we should do next. So that gets easier at some point. But at the same time, it becomes harder because of the potential arrogance of experience. I strongly encourage you to reflect on how this risk might apply to your practice.

***

Q41: How to make the change sustainable?

Coachees come to coaching to experience growth, achieve goals and solve some problems, with no intention of booking further sessions after the package ends. Right?

Yes, and... sharing the Jim Patterson quote once again, "We're not coaching for problems to be solved, but for lives to be lived". And the annoying thing with life is that it is constantly happening. One thing ticked off the list, and the next knocks on the door. Or am I the only one experiencing this...?

No, I am not a fan of having 'open end coaching relationships'! The maximum commitment I accept, generally, is six months. At the conclusion of each contract, we discuss whether the coachee wishes to continue the relationship and what both parties need to do to ensure its success. Officially called 'evaluation'.

When the coachee feels no need to continue the coaching relationship, for whatever reason, no hard feelings. When they do stop the coaching, the evaluation is part of the 'making it sustainable'. This is where you have a conversation about what it takes to ensure things don't slip through their fingers. This begins with looking at the original goals that brought them to coaching. What have they achieved and what have they learned about themselves? How did they get to where they find themselves now?

Metaphorically speaking, coaching is about giving our coachees an update to their 'Manual of Self'. When our coachee understands themselves better, knows what drives them, recognises the obstacles on their path they're most easily challenged by, they've won so much! When they embrace what they no longer want in their lives, and identify what they do want, something important has shifted within them. We are not coaching just for some change! All we do, the way we are, all is intended to evoke transformation. Transformation: 'an elemental shift in consciousness on the path of evolution'. This is something irreversible, just like the butterfly for whom it is impossible to return to a caterpillar. It is part of our job to support our coachee to see these lasting changes. To make them familiar with their updated 'Manual of Self'. The stronger their relationship with it and the stronger their commitment to keep tapping into it, the stronger they will show up when the next thing knocks on their door. Or when previous challenges repeat themselves.

Coaching can lead to sustainable results when the coachee keeps creating from their newly gained knowledge about themselves. And, when new challenges knock on their door, they might have learned enough to deal with them. Or they reconnect with their coach to add a few more pages to their 'Manual of Self', since this important document benefits from frequent updates.

***

Q42: How to quickly get to the essence?

Coachees come to a coaching session with a topic they'd like to explore. In all my years of coaching, I've never experienced anyone who started the session by saying *"My topic is my work and the way I currently see it is 'utterly boring'. I really could do with another perspective"*. Never!

It's usually nicely wrapped in a long story, with lots of details, all the characters in the story being described, what they did, said and maybe even how. And how something like this also happened a few months ago, leading to sleepless nights. That their partner is done with listening to their repetitive complaining and then said: *"Bring it to your coach, they are paid to listen to this kind of stuff"*. Just so you know...

Many coaches find it challenging to not use, or waste, too much time at the beginning of a session on trying to get clarity on what the topic is. There is this 'famous' 10-80-10 Roadmap for coaching which tells us we may only use 10% of the coaching time before we start the actual 'exploration' phase. Well, if you look at all we could, or even should, do in those first minutes of a session, good luck with that! I personally think this doesn't do justice to all we need to do before we take a deep dive into the topic.

Without going into the details of what the first part of a session could contain, there are a few things I'd like to address, to help you make the start of your coaching sessions more time efficient and effective.

A lot of the sharing many coachees like to do at the beginning of a session, is something they could write down and share prior to the session. This is not just a technique to buy time, because when someone writes things down, they usually learn more and come better prepared to a session. For these reasons I offer my coachees a journal and prepform where they can write down what they want, share their 'homework' and tell me what they feel like working on in the upcoming session. Aha, by thinking about what they want to work on in the upcoming session, they're already giving this some thought before the actual session. Remember, the coachee is responsible for the content, so let them do that work! This way their learning already begins even before the session.

For me, 'partnering' goes beyond the session, it also includes the preparation work both parties do before the session, making the process richer and more efficient.

And still, our coachees, like all of us, easily get lost in stories, thinking the coach needs to know all those details so they can better serve us. This is why we need to keep reminding them of the art of 'bottom-lining' and get to the essence of their topic. The story is only diverting their attention and reducing their learning.

It is part of our job to train our coachee in what it is to play their part in an efficient way as well as to give them context about why we want this for them. Coaching is about Exploration, not about Explanation, such as my first Golden Rule teaches, and they deserve to know and experience exactly that.

Referring to question 25 about the how and what of intruding, we need to practise that skill, otherwise this Golden Rule will not come to life. It's all about setting the context and designing the partnership. One of the things the coach can do is build a clear foundation under the session. The following five questions, as a structure, can be very helpful:
1: What do you want coaching on today?

When they go into too much detail:
2: What is the bottom line?

To start the peeling of the layers of the onion:
3: What is important to you about this topic?

If needed:
4: How do you relate to / feel about this topic?

To create a meta-view and to hold the focus:
5: What would be a good outcome of this session for you?

To make the sessions more effective, to get to the essence more quickly, we need to train our coachee and we need to dare to take charge over the process. Colleagues, don't shy away from this since it is in service to your coachee and their learning process.

***

Q43: What kind of coach are you?

There are two types of people in the world. Normal people, who don't know what coaching is about. And us coaches. Yes, we can't really say we're normal, compared to the rest of the world, can we?

We have funny habits, often speak a weird language, sometimes have a funny 'coach-voice'. We ask the strangest questions like "Where do you feel this in your body", or "What is the colour of that feeling?". As trained coaches, we can usually answer these kinds of questions; we speak our own language after all. It has become our second native tongue.

Yet, there is one question our coachees could ask that we find really hard to answer. It is a very powerful question. Suddenly, it seems as though our coachees have taken the same training! The question is short, open ended and they're freaking clueless about the answer.

The coach, too, will be sent on a journey of exploration by this question, often leaving them silent and speechless for a while. As if it is an inquiry; that powerful question on steroids, very short, multiple answers possible and often, with the answer barely found, the next question is already created.

Coachee, thank you very much for asking me "What kind of coach are you?"

You won't get away with saying you're a Co-Active coach or labelling yourself with whatever programme you were trained in. It won't make any sense to them and should you try, you will see that confused look on their face. You've got to come up with something better!

Okay, let's give it a try.

Coach: "I'm a life and career coach."
Coachee: "So you know everything about life and careers?"
Coach: "Uh, no. We trust you know all the answers yourself. We just ask questions to help you set that wisdom free..."
Coachee: "Uh... so you know nothing and I need to figure it out myself?"

Coach: “Uh, yes, glad you understand it...”
Coachee: “Thank you! That was very helpful...” (Not!)

We can replace the words ‘life and career’ with any other ‘specialty’, but the conversation will go more or less the same and will thus have a similar result. The coachee is confused and probably frustrated, and the coach is left feeling uncomfortable.

An alternative is that the coach claims to have a niche. This coach is specialised in working with people in a certain profession or environment, with a specific question. The expectation from the coachee, usually, is that the coach has specific knowledge they will share with them to find, or provide them with, their answer. This makes the coach the specialist and whilst coming from this expertise, what they become is a consultant or mentor. Nothing wrong with these two roles, it’s just not coaching.

Not coaching in the sense where we partner up with our coachees for a thought-provoking process to inspire them to maximise their personal and professional potential. When the coach sees the coachee as someone they do not need to help with the content, nor someone they need to provide any answers to. In other words, no need to fix them, rescue them, take care of them. They have what it takes!

Okay, this was just between you and me, dear colleague, because your coachee still doesn’t know anything more than they did when they asked the question the first time.

Before continuing, I must admit I struggled with this question for a long time myself! How the heck do we explain to normal people what kind of coach we are, without turning ourselves into some kind of specialist, something we just don’t want to be?

One of the most mind-blowing, magical things we have the privilege to witness, is that ‘lightbulb’ moment where our coachee all of a sudden sees their way forward. An opening, a different perspective. A shift in the emotional experience they have around a certain situation. When you see that surprise on their face, the sparkle in their eyes, that shift in posture or in the tone of their voice, that's when we know why we're doing this. Sometimes this can even move me to tears, tears of gratitude and a deep sense of joy.

When you re-read the paragraph above, that's where you find the answer to what kind of coach we are:
'A different way of looking at a topic'.
'Seeing a (new) way forward'.
'An aha moment'.
'A shift in their emotional experience'.

With none of the above, the topic we're coaching has changed! No, 'all' that shifted is their relationship with the topic. That is exactly what we do! All the tools and skills we have, all we do, the way we show up as a coach, has one purpose and one purpose only: to call forth an elemental shift in how the coachee relates to the topic. We sometimes call that transformation.

We're not coaching to solve the problem, we're coaching to shift the relationship the coachee has with the topic they bring to coaching.

From there, I can proudly say I am a 'relationship coach'!

***

Q44: How to manage Level 1 Listening?

As an outdoor guy, I often observe wildlife. I've learned that animals are often blessed with extremely well-developed senses. In order to survive, evolution gave some of them eyesight which totally disrespects darkness. They developed a night vision that makes a Navy SEAL very, very jealous.

Others can hear so clearly, it is as if they have the most high-tech microphones hanging a mile around them, enabling them to hear the softest sigh. Or their smell; the smallest breeze of wind makes it possible to pick up smells over a great distance. When I observe my dog when we go for a hike, it feels like she's reading a book whilst sniffing the tracks. She even seems to remember because the next time we're at that same place, she pays extra attention.

We also know that, for instance, whales and elephants can communicate over a huge distance through sound waves or vibrations in the ground. The list of mind-blowing examples is endless and often leaves us, the so-called highest developed species, feeling rather poorly equipped or even stupid. But actually, it's less dramatic than it may look at first sight. Comparing, or even competing with, other species is a rather pointless activity. Maybe, no, surely, we can learn a lot from how animals use their senses, yet there's something special about the human ability to listen.

In coaching land, listening is one of the core competencies we bring to the relationship. In coach training, we teach students that there are three levels of listening, but Stephen Covey and others distinguish five to seven levels of listening. For simplicity reasons, we'll just stick to three here. The International

Coach Federation (ICF) talks about 'Active Listening', the intention to be really present with our coachees. Most coaching schools speak about the three levels of listening as **internal** (Level 1), **focused** (Level 2) and **global** (Level 3). The bottom line being taught here is that we need to self-manage our **Level 1** listening because that's where we're busy with our own thoughts, ideas, solutions or even judgements. Since we accept that this is a normal human thing, we're kind to ourselves and say that as soon as we become aware of being in Level 1, we need to self-manage and go back to Level 2 and 3.

In **Level 2** we have a laser-focused attention on our coachee and everything they communicate. We do not only listen to their words, but also to the way they say something, their gestures, facial expressions, movements; everything they transmit, consciously or unconsciously. We like to describe that as being 'focused on the whole person', and we love to get curious about all of that. This is really cool, because our 'non-verbal communication' holds tons of information. Since we're often clueless about all these queues and what they're trying to tell us, playing it back to our coachee frequently leads to new awareness.

It gets even better when we include **Level 3**! That's when we include 'the vibe'. The vibe, the energy in the room, the energy around and between the coach and the coachee. Whether we're together in person or via a screen, it doesn't make a lot of difference, there's always a Level 3 to include and create from. It's really special and rich to include that in the coaching since many times the coachee isn't aware of this and when we share our observations with them, this too frequently leads to special insights.

So it's simple, right? We human beings can be at three levels of listening and we have the ability to choose at which level we want to be. Level 1 is wrong, Level 2 and 3 are the places to be as a coach. Easy! Yes, we could make it this simple, but with that kind of rigidity we miss a rich treasure... We look at our coachees as a whole person, where we, for instance, include the wisdom of not only the brain, but also the heart, the body and spirit. All these resources are to be included and created from.

The funny thing is that we coaches are as human as our coachees thus holding the same resources! All resources of the coach are an instrument for the coaching and when used consciously, potentially a huge gift for the coachee.

Our minds have thoughts and ideas which could serve the coachee.

Our hearts are a place of love and a well of wisdom. Why keep it from our coachees...?

Our bodies are constantly talking to us. A sudden nod in the stomach, a shiver down our back, goosebumps. Clearly information and very likely not meant for the coach. Thus for the coachee!

Our intuition, our 'gut formation' (some call it spirit) holds wisdom and surprises above and beyond logic. This is probably born in the relationship and Level 3 between the coach and the coachee. But it might reach the coach as a Level 1 awareness and we're encouraged to share that information with the rightful owner, the coachee.

Dear colleagues, our Level 1 is potentially a huge gift for our coachees so let's stop keeping that away from them since we think our Level 1 is wrong. As if it is not allowed to be part of the coaching.

Yes, keep your judgement and quick fixes out of the coaching. That form of Level 1 does not serve your coachees. All we coaches do, the way we are, is intended to call forth new awareness. And that's exactly the filter through which we need to test our Level 1! Is it not intended to call forth new awareness but instead to show how smart or kind we are? You, coach, need to get over that!

Is it a genuine gift, where we're unattached if the coachee wants to create from that gift? We might as well give it to them since it might be the breakthrough they needed. And you, with your Level 1 , were just the instrument for this.

We need to be consciously filtering our Level 1 to see if it passes this test. In addition, we need to reflect on how often we play this card.

Listening to our Level 1 thoughts all the time would impact the coaching in a non-supportive way. But if you do it consciously, maybe even after asking your coachee's permission for sharing this Level 1 experience, we can befriend our Level 1 as a rich tool that serves our coachees.

***

Q45: Do you have some tips for the Completion session?

Every coaching journey begins with a session where the coach and the potential coachee explore whether they are a match. This is really important and it's wise not to skip this since you're about to begin an important relationship. Both the coach and the coachee deserve this to be a very conscious decision. At the end of such a 'chemistry call', I always ask the other person to sleep on it for at least a night, even if they want to say 'Yes' right there and then. Borrowed from the book *The Prosperous Coach* the 'Yes' needs to be a 'Hell Yes!', or else it's a 'Hell No'! This means that 'Maybe' equals 'No'.

I want to underline that it takes a 'Hell Yes' from both coach and coachee since it happens too often that the coach finds it hard to say no to a potential coachee and, with that, they do themselves and their coachee a disservice. So, coach, dare to be honest and say 'No' when you are not convinced about the 'Hell Yes'!

Let's assume you are both enthusiastic and that you took the time to discuss a solid Designed Alliance so that both the coach and the coachee know what to expect, including the option to revisit this Designed Alliance. Most coaches have a specific way of doing the first session(s) where 'Discovery' work is being done. Explore values, goals, dreams, desired impacts in life, and any other elements the coach deems relevant. It's a great habit to do this rich Discovery work and create a strong foundation for the journey you are just about to begin.

At some point you come to the last agreed session. In general, coaches work with contracts in which they agree on a certain number of sessions and use the last session, or parts of it, to talk about this. At least, I hope you do take time for this and don't allow the relationship to come to an end, just like that.

In my early days I called this the 'Completion session'. Yet I started to dislike that word since the charge it has for me now, is that 'it's over'. I don't want to have the unintended impact that I don't want to work with them any more! So I changed the name to 'Evaluation session' and created an updated little questionnaire to help the coachee evaluate the journey up until that point. And unless one of us no longer feels the relationship is inspiring enough – because that's really the right moment to say goodbye – I start that conversation with both options wide open: we continue, or we wrap it up.

This means 'Evaluation' can become 'Completion', but it can also become the start of a new series of sessions. Both based on a conscious decision and an open conversation.

Wait, there is more. It's more than a conversation! It might be the last session in this coaching relationship, but it's still a coaching session. Since coaching is about taking our coachees on an adventurous journey of exploration, let's also do this in that session! Too often the last session turns into a pleasant conversation in which we exchange how much we appreciate each other and say goodbye in a warm way, potentially with the last words being "You're always welcome to come back!". Though it feels nice, it still feels like a missed opportunity...

How about looking at this last session as another 'Discovery' session, but this time it's based on what the coachee now knows about themselves and how they want to show up in life? Where we invite them for a 'helicopter-ride' and look back on the coaching sessions from a distance in order to see the big picture. What happened, how have I been, what have I achieved?

Then let the helicopter just hover for a moment so that the coachee can look at today, at this moment. To see, from a distance, how their life looks and ask them how that feels.

The next thing is to turn the helicopter around so the coachee can look into the future, where the coach is wildly curious about what they see. Or want to see. Maybe there are new dreams waking up on the horizon? From this meta view, we check in with our coachee whether they feel they could do with ongoing coaching. They already experienced the magic of coaching and how that supports them to get more out of their life and to live it in a more conscious way, and there's a fair chance they are eager to continue the partnership with you, their coach.

The bottom line: Use the last scheduled session as another chance to explore and discover. Let it be coaching!

Below you will find some questions you could include in this session or in a short questionnaire you ask your coachees to complete prior to this session.

Possible questions for an Evaluation questionnaire:

- What have you achieved as a result of the coaching?
- What are your top five values at this moment?
- What do you see as the next thing for you?
- What Limiting Beliefs did you let go of?
- What Supporting Beliefs do you now own?

- What are important things you learned about yourself?
- What is today's version of your Life Purpose Statement?
- How does that inform your daily choices?
- Who do you see as your Personal Support Team?
- How do they support you on a daily basis?
- What has been the best part of the coaching for you?
- What tips or feedback do you have for me as your coach?
- Do you wish to continue our coaching? (Yes / No / Later)
- If yes, what are the main goals you want to work on?
- If yes, what needs to be adjusted in our partnership?

***

Q46: What's the difference between Acknowledgement and Championing?

It was at secondary school. I was 13 and dealing with my second bone fracture in just a few months. You can probably picture these kids, doing their best to quickly grow up whilst trying to carry their way too big bag with all their books and other school materials. Combine that with a broken arm and you're probably not the most elegant version of yourself.

On that day, I was walking through the huge school building and had to go through one of the heavy doors. One arm broken, with the other carrying my bag. And I had to be fast, as I was already running late for the next class. So, somewhat stressed and in order to get through the door, I put my foot against the bottom part of it and pushed it open. Worked like a charm! Guess what, there was one person who had a different perspective on my creative action... the Principal of the school...

The Principal stopped me and yelled at me and 'asked' me if something was wrong in my head (schools were a bit less 'sensitive' back in those days...). Assuming it was a genuine question and that he may have a problem with his eyesight, I replied with, "No, sir, nothing wrong with my head, my arm is broken". I couldn't understand why he exploded and sent me to his office where I got lectured as if I'd just destroyed the school. His school. I must have done something really bad since I didn't just get a warning, not even a 'yellow card'; no, this action deserved a 'red card'. At my football club, I was too young to be corrected with a red card, yet here I wasn't.

I felt unjustly treated and not seen. I was dismissed, and he didn't take anything but his own frustration into consideration. This left a small mark on my young and sensitive heart, otherwise why else would I still remember it?

Though not the biggest fan of football any more, the other day something in the news caught my eye. Something unique happened since the article wasn't about a yellow card or a red card: the referee gave someone a 'white card'. Where the other two colours serve to punish unwanted behaviour, this white card was not a punishment but an acknowledgement, in order to promote fair play during the match! What a wonderful, different way of thinking! Instead of punishing behaviour, this card puts the focus on the opposite. Instead of the referee calling the player to them, where the player has to partake in a walk of shame and whilst standing in front of the referee one of the two cards will be shown, here the referee goes to the person to underline they have been seen for how they behaved. The white card serves to honour the person and to make the public statement that this behaviour deserves to be celebrated, seen and respected.

I see you.
I respect you.
I celebrate you.
I acknowledge you.

In coaching we have the same skill: Acknowledgement. The same four sentences are applicable. The coach puts words on how the coachee was 'being', usually in a short sentence like, "You are courageous making this choice".

Frequently, it's not easy for our coachees to hear such words. In the world out there, we are used to yellow and red cards. Society is using these 'correction methods' frequently, where the 'corrector' is prosecutor, judge and executor. Without any form of trial.

We harden ourselves not to get hurt each time this happens to us. We just think 'whatever', turn around and try to move on. Just toughen up and get over it! By toughening up, we are building a wall around our hearts, intended to protect ourselves. However, that wall isn't only blocking all that negative stuff, it also blocks the love and warmth that comes with an Acknowledgement from entering our hearts. This is exactly what happens with our coachees and often they wave our Acknowledgements away, because they can't be with it.

Just think about this for a while. Do you recognise this?

And I observe something else as well. It's not only the coachee for whom receiving Acknowledgements is hard –many coaches also have a hard time giving or receiving them. They either use no Acknowledgements in their coaching or they only give one brief one at the end, as if it were a necessary box to tick to make your coaching good coaching.

Just think about this for a while. Do you recognise this?

I see Acknowledgements as 'balm to our hearts': they make us glow and believe in ourselves more. They help build self-confidence and form an invitation to step into the best version of ourselves. So we can't be generous enough with them.

It can get even better and more supportive. Coaches work with their coachees whilst seeing their magnificence and, at the same time, hold a powerful vision for them. The coach sees things that are waiting for the coachee that the coachee does not dare to see themselves. The skill of 'Championing' is where the coach cheers their coachee for what they believe is about to happen. As if the coach already celebrates the coachee finishing a marathon whilst the race only starts next week. The coach has zero doubt that the coachee will show up as their best self: they won't be surprised at all if the coachee does way better than they themselves expected.

Championing is like giving them wind beneath their wings so they can fly to greater heights. The combination of these two skills has a very powerful impact on the coachee. Where the Acknowledgement gives words to how they are being now, Championing is future oriented and full of belief in what the coachee is about to become. Who are you being now, who you are becoming tomorrow? One hand massaging the heart, the other a gentle push in the back. This is an environment where yellow and red cards aren't part of the game, since coaching is a judgement-free environment. There are more than enough self-appointed judges in the world, for sure our coachees don't need their coach to be another one. Instead, the coach is generous with white cards to acknowledge their coachee whilst sprinkling some 'pixie dust' over them to underline their magic.

Just think about this for a while. How generous are you with white cards and pixie dust?

You have a heart filled with love for your coachees; let it speak.

You are a faithful supporter of your coachees, make them spread their wings so they will fly!

Wow, think about this for a while... what a cool job we have...

COACH

***

Q47: Who is in the lead in coaching?

The first Golden Rule for Coaching I speak about in my previous book is the following one: "Coaching is about exploration, not about explanation". We want to offer our coachees a rich journey of exploration, take them on a scavenger hunt. We want them to discover a new world of possibilities and from there start to make self-empowering choices that lead to a more conscious life. Making the best of life, being a leader over their choices and not a victim of circumstances. We want to avoid them explaining to us what they already know. You know, all those events from the past–the actions others took or failed to take, the attempts they made, or the reasons they believe things are unchangeable. All this explanation leads to nothing new, because they are already familiar with it.

Instead, we want them to take a look at new possibilities, where they honour what they stand for, believe in, live for. New perspectives that open up a completely new point of view on a certain situation and all of a sudden, they feel more is possible than they could see till then. Our longing for them is that they dare to make choices that make their heart sing. That they explore feelings they might have avoided for years and with that set themselves free from limitations. Talking about limitations: when we see them shed a limiting belief, our own heart also sings. Bottom line, there's lots and lots of good stuff that can come from a coaching relationship and the way the coach shows up in it.

Based on our training, we have a variety of skills and tools we can use to support the coaching process.

Borrowing from one of the ICF ways to describe coaching: we partner with our coachees for a creative and thought-provoking process to inspire them to optimise their personal and professional potential. Creative and thought-provoking. Let's take a look at those words, with a special focus on the 'thought-provoking' part. How do we show up to 'provoke thoughts' so our coachees can tap into their potential? How do we have to be so they allow themselves to step into that? What do we have to do to encourage them to take a look beyond what they saw as possible until then?

One thing is that we have to practise curiosity. Not to feed our own need to know, but in order for them to explore new terrain, as mentioned before. We can use our intuition, that knowledge above and beyond logic. Offer it unfiltered to them, and simply wait and see what they create from it.

We are listening at a deep level to all they communicate. We focus not only on their actual words, but also on how they say them. We even include the energy, the vibe in the space and the vibe between the coach and the coachee. We want them to learn about themselves and translate that knowledge into actions they experiment with outside of the coaching session. Therefore, we need to self-manage our thoughts, smart ideas or solutions. With a bit of luck, we even dare to be 'lazy coaches' that trust our coachees so much that we allow them to do most of the work.

With this as our 'way of being' whilst coaching, we of course also have a toolkit filled with 'toys and tricks' we can use during the coaching. I mean, we have many professional tools we can use to provoke these new thoughts. Forgive me for not being so serious for a moment!

One of the most common skills for coaches is asking questions. There are several basic rules around these questions. For instance, they need to be open ended. We try to avoid 'why-questions'. Impactful questions are usually rather short and invite the coachee to go and explore things from a new angle. Okay, since we agreed to be serious, let's take it to the next level! Our questions also need to be so open and genuinely curious that we are clueless as to where our coachee will be taking this. We need to be surprised to hear what comes out of our own mouth when we ask a question. In other words, we need to avoid 'leading questions'. Let's repeat this: no leading questions!

A leading question is a question where we know our coachee is going to think and respond in a certain way. A leading question comes with a plan. It's when we think we know better than our coachee and start to play the smart-ass. That is NOT our job as a coach and it is not in line with what the ICF describes as coaching.

I can almost hear you think: "I don't do that"! Let's agree, this is not you, but let me share a little secret: I sometimes have a weak moment and when I then look back at a session, I realise I didn't live up to my own expectations. I couldn't help starting to think... Oops! I so often say that 'thinking is not a coaching skill', and now I did it myself. Even though I always preach that we need to let the coachee find their own way, in hindsight I must confess that that one question was maybe, okay, surely, pointing in a certain direction. I must admit that I did it in a very 'smart' way since the coachee didn't even notice it! Actually, that's making it even worse...

The problem is that we want so badly for our coachees to find their way forward, that we sometimes forget to self-manage our enthusiasm. Not a mortal sin yet not very professional at the same time. It is not our job to show them where the door towards their way forward is. It is not our job to take them by the hand and lead them towards a solution. Because when we do, there's a fair chance they will follow our lead. However subtle. In fact, the more subtle the lead, the bigger the chance they will not notice and simply choose that path. This can happen, it probably happens to all of us, so we need to keep checking in with ourselves and notice when we get too enthusiastic and start leading the way. Instead, we need to give our coachees as much space as possible to find their own way. Let them go where they lead themselves.

Deal?

***

Q48: What are coaches actually selling?

Coaches are often primarily driven by their love for people. By a big heart that wants nothing but the best for their coachees. Many coaches claim they would still do this even if they didn't get paid for it, so big is the intrinsic motivation and reward.

You feel the 'but' coming, right? There are multiple reasons why coaching – in general – should not be given for free. First of all, professional coaches have seriously invested in their education in coaching. You deserve to earn this back.

Coaches also bring lots of additional life experience; you deserve to be rewarded for this. And then we have the practical part: that coaches simply need to make a living; you deserve a decent income from the professional services you provide.

Additionally, we have learned that coachees who pay a good fee for their coaching, are generally more engaged and willing to put in the work. Wait a minute, the coachee needs to 'put in the work'? Isn't it the coach who is working and the coachee who is receiving a service?

I'd word it like this: the coach is at work. At work, the coach creates an inspiring, safe and courageous environment. In that environment, the coachee is encouraged to go on a scavenger hunt of self-exploration. The better the coach, the less they work. Yes, the better the coach, the less they work and the lazier they dare to be in their coaching! In my book *Golden Rules for Coaching*, I claim that working is not a coaching skill, laziness is.

So, as coaches, we work as little as possible – all we do is create that really special space and let our coachees do the work? And we dare to charge for this? How on earth can I sell this to my prospects? Oh, to make it even more challenging, we do not guarantee any results. We don't, because we believe that the results mainly depend on how willing the coachee is to do their part.

Between coaches, we can probably explain how this works. To use some Co-Active language: we are responsible for the evoking, the coachee for the transformation. But how can we explain that to a 'normal person', someone who is new to coaching? How do you answer when they ask what they will get as a result from partnering with you? It might be a bit vague for them when we say that the result they will experience is 'transformation'. They will probably be even more confused when we say we sell 'evoking'... Even though, essentially, that is what we do when we partner with them for a creative and thought-provoking process to inspire them to optimise their professional and personal potential, as per the ICF description of coaching.

Creative and thought-provoking. Optimising potential. The potential is already present in the coachee. We call forth a new way of thinking, a new way of looking at themselves and the world around them. We encourage our coachees to tap into their creativity and, with that, live towards the life they want to experience. When we invite our coachees to start exploring their potential, they frequently say they want this, but are unsure how to proceed. It is exactly what they are longing for, yet they've never been able to find the way to get there. This is why we take them on a journey of self-exploration and self-discovery.

Imagine you buy a new TV. One of those super modern TVs with endless possibilities: they are so brilliant they are called 'smart-TVs'. For me personally, that usually leads to me not feeling so smart at all... Optimistic as I am, I just plug it in, turn it on and then expect it to understand what I want it to do. Hey, is it a smart-TV or what!? Well, it doesn't often work like that. Bummer, I need to work through the freaking manual of about 1,000 pages. First, I need to find the language I understand best, then I actually need to understand what I am reading. Frequently this leads to a quarrel with my wife, some language that I'd better not repeat here, and tons of frustration. I just spent all that money on this TV and now I need to spend even more to hire a specialist to get the TV going and teach me how to use it.

This is a pretty cool metaphor for the process our coachees go through. They are like a smart-TV with tons of potential, but without a manual, that potential won't be unlocked. There are a few differences though. We human beings do not come with an already written manual. We can't download it from the web, nor Google it. We can't even ask our parents. Sorry! The second difference is that we can't hire a specialist to write it for us and then explain to us how to use it. Sorry.

This is where the coach comes in: we offer a process where the coachee can start writing their own manual. It will probably be a first draft with lots of space to add an appendix here and there. And with that first draft, the coachee needs to go and experiment. In other words, after writing their 'Manual of Self', the coachee needs to learn how to apply what's written there. We need to encourage them to just give it a go because it'll be like AI, it'll get better and better with experience. Better, easier to read, more complete, easier to apply. And in this case, AI doesn't stand for 'Artificial Intelligence', but rather 'Authentic Intelligence'.

Going back to the starting question, what is it that we are selling to our coachees? We sell them a 'Manual of Authentic Intelligence'.

***

Q49: What's a good way to structure our sessions?

Many coaches have previous experience leading projects in their professional or private lives. Every project has a beginning: the current situation. You start a project with a certain desired outcome in mind and in between the current situation and the desired outcome, some work needs to be done. When the project is done, you start implementing the results so you can benefit from the hard work and all the thinking that you have done. After the results of the project have been integrated, new insights are often created or circumstances changed. And there you go, an update is needed, maybe even a completely new project. Nothing strange so far?

The question is, why don't we treat our coaching sessions the same way? We're working on someone's most important project – their life – and due to a lack of structure, we allow the coaching sessions to stay on the level of a 'nice conversation'? As part of our professional, and even ethical, responsibility we need to take charge and create a clear structure for our coaching sessions. Some call it the 10/80/10, others the roadmap for coaching, and here I will simply call it 'the structure'. The importance lies not in the name but in the game, so let's go and play!

A coaching session needs a clear beginning, followed by a big phase of exploration and discovery, and towards the end we wrap up by collecting the lessons learned and planning some specific actions. Let's take a closer look at the different phases of a well-structured coaching session.

Getting grounded

This is how I see the start of a coaching session. Our coachees have many things going on in life and often we're just one of the many meetings they have in their busy schedule. We need to slow down for a moment and understand which version of our coachee we're meeting at that moment, get aligned and clarify what they want to focus on and achieve in this session. The ingredients, not always in that order, for the 'Getting grounded' phase are the following:

Checking in: Welcoming our coachees to the session and ask how they are being. No, that's not a mistake, I consciously don't say 'how they are doing'! If you ask them how they are doing, that question is either answered with 'fine' or you get a list of all the things they are busy with. 'Fine' stands for 'Feelings I'm Not Expressing' and they don't come to coaching to share their to-do list. Instead, we need to get a feel for who the person is, how they are feeling. Connect with them, with their whole self. A way to do this is by asking them to complete the following sentences with just a few words:

My mind is...
My body is...
My heart is...
My spirit is...
My life is...

Clearing: During check-in, the coachee may feel the need to get something off their chest. It's not the topic they want to explore, but it's something that weighs on their mind or heart. Usually it is 'simply' the day-to-day things like a sick pet, a silly argument, an unexpected invoice. By sharing this, they clear their emotions and clean up the energetic space to get them ready for exploring the actual topic.

Accountability: Most likely, they left the previous session with some specific actions they decided to work on. Coachees often choose to share the results and insights they got from these actions, so make sure not to forget this. Go straight for the learning and new awareness they got from it and avoid the story!

Designed Alliance: As an essential ethical pillar under our profession, we have the habit of consciously discussing with our coachees how we both want to show up in this coaching relationship in order to make it a safe space where each of us can show up fully.

This is not something we only do at the very beginning of the coaching relationship, we need (!) to ask about the Designed Alliance at the beginning of each session. We cannot assume that all is fine and clear. And when we want to try out something new with our coachee, we even need to design that during the session. Do not assume that all is clear and okay.

Topic: We're 'finally' at the point where we can ask what topic(s) the coachee wants to explore in this session. Since this is usually leading to the coachee telling us a story with too much detail, we have to take charge and intrude. Not to cut them off, but to help them get to the essence in their words. In order to get a feeling for how the coachee relates to the topic and how to start the exploration phase, we can ask them the following questions:
- What is important to you about this topic?
- How do you feel about this?

Desired outcome: We want our coachees to walk away from the session with something tangible, and we want to avoid drifting away from this during the session, so we need to ask them what 'success at the end of the session' would look like. This makes them co-responsible for the session. It is one of the ways to actually 'partner up' with them. At the same time, this question creates a meta view we can hold on to and refer back to during the session.

Before we move on to the next phase, just a little side note. Look at all I've listed above! If you feel you need to squeeze that in 10% of the coaching session, let's say that's six minutes, you might end up disappointed because this hardly ever works. These are essential ingredients that cannot be skipped or rushed through. Without a solid foundation, the building will not stand firmly. Dare to give it the time and space it deserves, whilst at the same time taking charge to keep things moving. Nice paradox, right?

Exploration

We're now ready to start the biggest part of the session, the exploration phase. This is where we spend 60-80% of the coaching time. This is where we explore multiple ways of looking at the same situation, where the coachee experiences resonance or dissonance, the emotions they experience around this topic. This is where we help our coachees connect with who they are at their core and how they can make self-empowering choices from there, rather than being driven by circumstances or what the world around them says they need to do.

Too many of us, too often, allow circumstances or the people around us to choose for us. Our longing for our coachees is that they tap into their own full potential and design their life, consciously, from there.

Co-Active coaches use the three Principles in the exploration phase, creating new awareness by using the tools and skills that come with these Principles. 'Fulfillment' reconnects the coachee with what they really want, 'Balance' with the power of choice, and 'Process' with embracing being fully alive and giving ourselves permission to experience all our feelings. In question 58 I will take a closer look at these Principles.

Insights and Action

At some point, the clock will be telling us it is time to wrap up the coaching session. Yes, watching the clock is a coaching skill and it is a sign of professionalism to respect the agreed time for the session. And 'Taking Charge' is a coaching skill we need to apply in all three phases of the coaching session. When you see the time is almost up, simply announce: "It is almost time for us to wrap up our session. What have you learned so far about the topic we explored?".

These two sentences are the bridge between the exploration phase and the last part of the session where we collect insights and translate them into a specific action. We can ask our coachees what action they feel like taking or we can suggest an action for them. When we offer them an action, it needs to be a genuine offer which they can take, adjust or deny. We can either request them to do something 'doable', a challenge to step into a serious stretch, or ask them to reflect on something, often described as an inquiry. And 'Inquiry' is a powerful question on steroids that deserves to marinate over time.

In order to help them not forget about the action they chose to take, we can brainstorm a structure as a reminder. This might be an image on their phone, a sticky note on the mirror or a stone in their pocket.

Ultimately, it's less about the actions they take and more about the learning and new awareness that come from it. Therefore, we tailor the type of accountability that will best support them. This is not about reporting back to the coach, nor is it about how well they did their 'homework'. It's all about the new awareness! Have a look at the Awareness Cycle in my book *Golden Rules for Coaching* if you're looking for a nice image for this. Before sending them off into their lives again, don't forget to celebrate them and their learning.

In Appendix 3 you'll find your cheat sheet. Don't tell anyone 😉

***

Q50: Do we really have to ask about the Designed Alliance in every coaching session?

Going for your MCC-credentials is a big thing. The fact that you've collected so many hours of coaching experience, at least 2,500, is a huge achievement in itself. For most of us, this is years and years of coaching, always combined with ongoing coach education and mentoring. After first celebrating the ACC and PCC milestones, you finally feel ready to go for the highest ICF-credentials in our profession: Master Certified Coach (or its Association for Coaching equivalent, which is a very similar achievement).

Probably after some time of procrastination and dealing with your Saboteurs, you decide to ask another Master Coach to guide you through this intense experience.

I personally clearly remember how much it took to get to this point, to get over myself and give it my best. I must admit, the coaching I did for this process was probably not the best, the most authentic I've ever done. As part of the exam, you need to share two recordings where you need to tick all the boxes. All the markers need to be present. Whilst in this process, you talk with colleagues who have already done it, and they share their experiences. I still remember one of them very clearly. A highly experienced, highly respected colleague shared that she failed the exam because of one thing. Just one of the markers was missing. A detail, one could say.

This coach did everything in line with the markers and the coaching was good and impactful. The only thing missing was checking if the partnership, the Designed Alliance, needed to be refreshed in any way. In her defence, the coach shared that she had been working with this coachee for a long time, that they knew each other so well that the Designed Alliance was clear and solid. The examiners underlined that we can never assume, however well we might know each other, that the partnership doesn't need adjustment or fine tuning. We always need to check with our coachees, in each and every session.

This became a very important lesson for me and even though I dare to rebel against rules, this is one rule I've chosen to embrace. Reflecting on this, I started to see multiple layers here. It became even more clear to me when I applied this principle to my personal relationships, my marriage in particular. At some point, my wife and I found ourselves in a downward spiral because we didn't talk enough about our needs in this relationship. We drifted apart, to the point of almost ending up in a divorce. We almost lost our marriage, because we did not consciously invest time in re-designing what we needed from this relationship. Bit by bit we worked our way back and we're now stronger than ever before. The lesson: talk and re-design. Over and over. Don't start assuming or taking things for granted.

Since coaching is also about being in a very specific relationship, it's the exact same thing! In order to keep the coaching relationship fresh and inspiring, and to respect the needs of both the coachee and the coach, we need to keep going back to the drawing board. Like in any relationship, it is not just a box to tick. If we only inquire about our partner's needs at the start of the year, we can expect challenges to arise as the year progresses. Simply because circumstances change, needs change, the individual changes. I know that's totally clear to you, but how often do you actually check in with your partner about their needs? Take this as a bonus question...

I'm using this obvious example to make it even more clear that it works the same way in a coaching relationship. We simply can't assume that talking about this at the very beginning is enough. We need to keep checking in with each other.

Over time, I've learned that even addressing the Designed Alliance at the beginning of a coaching session isn't always enough. Let's imagine the coaching relationship is safe and strong enough that the coachee is okay with bringing an emotionally charged topic. Maybe they don't even do it consciously, they 'just' bring something to the session and it's the coach who picks up the hidden emotions in the coachee's words, gestures or facial expressions. Maybe it's the intuition of the coach telling them that there's more going on. It's a courageous act from the coach to address that and to create a space where it's okay to explore these stuck emotions. Yet: let's not assume it's indeed okay for the coachee to go down that path. We need to ask their permission first, and asking permission is in essence a moment of fine-tuning the Designed Alliance.

Another example is when the coach feels the urge to get up and start moving around during the session. In their enthusiasm, or because they've done this before, the coach might assume it's also okay this time. Well, how do you know...?

Or when the coach feels like doing a specific exercise, let's say a visualisation. Visualisations are great and have proven to be very effective for many coachees. But (!) not always and not for everyone. Even if you've done this before with this coachee, how do you know they're okay with it in this session, in this moment?

Just as you strive to be respectful towards your partner or friends, extend that same respect to your coachees! Most of us are familiar with the somewhat naughty additional meaning of the word 'assume'. When we break it up into ass-u-me, it holds a message that we don't want for our coachees or ourselves. We therefore need to keep maintaining and nurturing this empowering relationship. We need to keep fine-tuning it so that both the coach and the coachee remain equally responsible for this. It's the oil that smooths the relationship and the glue that binds it.

From the start up right until the end: it's all in the design!

***

Q51: How to manage our own Saboteurs after being hired to coach someone?

Each time we get a new coachee, it brings a smile to our face, doesn't it! The excitement of starting a new adventure with a wonderful human being, what a privilege! The fact you're trusted enough by this person, is another thing that means a lot. And of course, let's admit, it also helps when we can make a living out of something we're so passionate about: coaching.

In my early days I was often a bit scared, wondering if I was good enough to serve this person. Would the coaching be impactful enough? Would it be worth the money? Would they speak positively about me, about my coaching?

Good old Saboteur, you so often tried to ruin the party... By now I understand you were just nervous about the change that you knew was about to happen, and that it was your job to try and hinder that. I'm glad that, in the meantime, I've been able to find other things, other places to keep you busy.

One way this Saboteur tried to get under my skin was by telling me I had to start with explaining the model I was using for my coaching. I remember sessions where I put the model on the table and gave a little lecture. An attempt to convince the coachee I knew what I was doing? That it all made sense and that there was a lot of knowledge behind all of this? It now makes me smile when I remember the confused look on my coachee's face.

I'm not talking about setting context for what we're asking our coachees to do with us. If we're, for instance, introducing how we can use the wisdom of the body during the coaching, and we do not give context for the purpose of that, the coachee might simply resist it because they don't get the point. Or when we want to explore certain emotions and we just drag our coachee into that, that could lead to a wonderfully failed session and a coachee resisting the coaching. No, we need to train our coachees in what it takes for them to play the game. We wouldn't start a board game without looking at the rules, why would we do it in coaching?

However, this serves merely as a tool to assist the coachee during the coaching process, it's not the essence of coaching nor what they come to coaching for. In reality, the coachees really don't care at all what kind of a model we're trained in, nor do they usually want to fully understand all the things we're doing. First of all, they trust you know what you're doing – so why wouldn't you trust yourself? Secondly, they only want to feel safe when you ask them to do certain exercises during the coaching session. They will feel safe because, returning to the previous statement, they trust you and, moreover, have a basic understanding of what you're asking from them. It's as simple as that! So, we can now stop worrying about all that Saboteur driven shit which we can describe as 'showing off'. Instead of showing off, we'd better show up! Show up as yourself! Yes, as you!

The coach is a unique instrument for the coaching experience. The coach as a human being, with all they've got, with all they are. In the chemistry call we have with our potential coachees, they mainly try to get a sense for how they feel about us. It's like a first date. A first experience of the energy of an unfamiliar human being. The potential coachee is often a bit unsure and trying to find their way in all of this. Whether they are looking for a coach by their own choice, or were encouraged to do so by their employer, they are curious about the human being they're going to meet. Will they click with you? Will they trust you? Will they like you? Will what they've heard about you be in line with their own experience? Because trust me, our previous and existing coachees love to 'brag' about their coach! We all know word of mouth is the best marketing imaginable; well, that's exactly what happens! Our coachees are spreading the word for us in their network and that's how we (eventually) get most of our new coachees. So, in most cases, the chemistry call is about not much more than them getting a confirmation of what they've already heard about you. If the 'gossip' is true.

If you were to ask your previous and current coachees what they most appreciate about you, they usually won't say that you were a master in applying a certain model. Though I love and respect it very much, not even the Co-Active Model 😉 They wouldn't mention how powerful your questions were, nor how metaphorical your metaphors. Not that you are a CPCC, a PCC or even an MCC. They just don't care very much about any of that!

They will speak about how you showed up.

About how you are as a human being.

About how much they felt heard, seen and supported by you.

How authentic you were.

How you dared to be you, so they could be – and further explore – themselves as well.

Let me say this in the Alex way: they hire YOU, not your training nor your credentials. So be YOU, because it's YOU who gets hired.

***

Q52: What's the magic of Co-Active coaches?

Some of the magic of Co-Active Coaching is experienced through the depth of how we explore the topic the coachee brings to the coaching. Once I've spent some time checking in with the coachee to discuss their experiences since our last session and clarify which topic they want to explore during this session, the deep dive can begin.

The Co-Active coach has many different coaching skills available, and when used at the right moment, they will have a powerful impact on the coachee. We've all seen what happens to the coachee when they hear the 'million dollar question'. It can take their breath away for a moment, it can make the scales drop from their eyes. It can wake them up, call out their BS, change things completely for them. The image we offer them, in the form of a metaphor, might unexpectedly make them see a clear picture. Or when we articulate back to them that we noticed a shift in their tone of voice, and then get curious about it. From there, they know they can't hide it any more, whatever 'it' may be.

The list goes on and we've seen magic happen in front of our eyes. Where other coaching approaches stop here, the Co-Active Model has lots more to offer! We can deepen the learning a lot further and we can create even more deeply rooted insights for our coachees when we use the powerful tools and skills embedded in the Principles. There are multiple ways to describe what a Principle in Co-Active coaching is. I like to see them as a 'doorway into exploration'. When we take our coachees through these doors, they can claim back their dreams, reconnect with the power of choice, and rediscover the fullness of life again. Take a moment to re-read the previous sentence:

reclaim dreams, the power of choice, experience life fully. What a privilege to witness our coachees on such a special journey!

All this sounds great and maybe also a bit 'by the book', so let's move away from this for a moment. What if we were to ask what Harry Potter, or another magician, had to say about how to add magic to your coaching? The answer is the same for them as it is for us! It's your *range* that decides how magical your coaching can become.

There is a popular Facebook group for coaches with the inspiring words 'kick ass' in the group name. Let's start with asking how much ass you actually dare to kick in your coaching? How often do you actually dare to play BIG, dear colleague? How far do you dare to colour outside the lines?

We've entered an era where what is considered 'appropriate' in coaching is often more about political correctness than adhering to ethical rules. 'Yes' to the ethical guidelines as provided by the International Coaching Federation (ICF), which push our profession to high standards. I fully support and strive to respect these high standards. But I say 'No' to what others tell me is appropriate in coaching. This would mean that 'appropriate' is what the average coach thinks. As we all know, the 'average coach' does not exist, at least I hope not...

When 'average' doesn't really exist, the definition of what is perceived as 'appropriate' also becomes rather vague, doesn't it?

Merriam Webster describes 'appropriate' as: "assigned to a particular purpose or use". So that means it depends on the situation. This means we need to be sensitive to what our coachee needs, or better said, 'deserves' in a certain situation. Sometimes our coachee deserves for us to simply be silent and hold a sacred space. Sometimes our coachee deserves for us to hit our fist on our desk and call out their BS. Sometimes we create a metaphorical environment to explore the deepest emotions. Sometimes we dance around the room to explore what it is to be happy and alive.

Sometimes we're a saint, sometimes we're the black sheep. In an inspiring, full out, no handbrake, cut the crap, get real, love to bits, fight for growth coaching relationship, there is space for both the saint and the black sheep. People don't come to coaching for sugarcoating. People don't come to coaching to be bored by the sessions. People don't want coaching to be predictable. People don't expect coaches to have a funny 'coach voice' that is very different from their normal voice. We encourage our coachees to be real and authentic, so let's model that in how we show up as the coach! Authentic means "true to one's own personality, spirit or character" (quoting Merriam Webster again). Building on that, depending on the situation, our personality, our spirit, our character will show up in specific ways. Sometimes we're calm and warm, sometimes we're on fire. We switch from being happy and full of love, to being like a thunderstorm.

This is exactly what our coachees deserve to get from us! Based on the flow of the session, or even the relationship, they should be able to expect us to show up real and raw. Pure and authentic. A coaching relationship turns into something magical when the coach dares to play full out, knowing the coachee so well, trusting the relationship so much that they show up with all they've got. As though it's an improv class where one needs to create from whatever the other throws at you. Not to please them, not simply to be nice, but to be genuine and engage in a mesmerising dance together. Sometimes fast, sometimes slow. Sometimes laid back, sometimes full of passion and fire. Feels like being real and fully alive, doesn't it...?

So, dear coaches:
Dare to be an angel, dare to be a devil.
Dare to encourage, dare to call out BS.
Dare to be the best friend, dare to be the black sheep.
Dare to be what your coachee and their growth is asking for in that moment.
Dare to be the range your coachee deserves to create magic.

***

Q53: Can coaches become addicted to coaching for the mental satisfaction or self-fulfillment?

Another amazing question offered by a dear colleague and I really had to sit with this for a while before finding my answer.

The short answer is: Addicted? Nah, not really. Developing a certain dependency feels like a possible risk though.

Let me give you a bit more than just that. I take the topic of addiction very seriously and I believe that any one of us can become an addict, in many different ways, to many different substances. To check my own thoughts about what something is, or what a word means, I like to check what the Merriam Webster dictionary has to say. I have never seen a coach who showed symptoms like anxiety, irritability or nausea when their substance (coaching) was taken away from them. So in that sense, addiction is not applicable and even using the word 'substance' feels like taking it too far.

With addiction, something changes in our brain, because *"repeated exposure to an addictive substance or behaviour causes nerve cells in the nucleus accumbens and the prefrontal cortex to communicate in a way that couples liking something with wanting it, in turn driving us to go after it"*. (source 'The Sapien Medicine Community'). I do not believe this could be created by coaching other people.

When I look at another part of the definition, I think there is a risk though that coaches could develop a not so healthy behaviour. I wouldn't call it addiction but rather the development of a habit where we become dependent on the dopamine we feel when we coach someone. Dopamine is created in our brain when we experience something really nice, like eating, sports or sex. It gives us an experience of joy, pleasure or even euphoria. So far, nothing wrong with that.

The description of addiction also mentions a certain compulsive behaviour. For some enthusiastic coaches, especially those who have just discovered coaching, it may seem that way since they try to coach anyone at any time. No worries, your environment will cure you quickly!

The only risk I see is when coaches become dependent on coaching itself, seeking their self-worth through the act of coaching others. This is probably the case for other professionals as well. Many of us confuse 'what we do' with 'who we are'. I know, coaching someone and seeing the magic happen for them can make us feel really happy and fulfilled. Yes, you contributed to that process BUT you didn't do this! We must keep remembering that it's always the coachee who makes the choices that lead them to that magic. It is their transformation, not ours. We simply called it forth by providing an environment where they can tap into their potential. Though we do care for them, we didn't cure them.

Turn it around and imagine that your coachee makes a choice that doesn't make you so happy. Or that they do not choose at all. Maybe such a coaching process is less fulfilling for you personally, but it doesn't define you. It is not sustainable nor healthy when we try to find our self-worth in our job. A job is a job, no matter how beautiful or important it is. It is and will always be something that you do, and not who you are. An external thing. Self-worth, as the term implies, can only be found in self.

***

Q54: How to coach someone in grief?

There are colleagues who are specialised in this, and in all honesty, I am not. The gift in coaching coming from the Co-Active Model, is that you can coach more or less any topic. While it's important to distinguish between coaching and therapy, which serve different purposes, I believe that for most people experiencing grief, often it isn't accompanied by a traumatic event that would require therapeutic support.

Grief is both the most painful and beautiful human emotion. Intense grief will only exist when there is intense love. When we grieve, at the same time we honour the deep connection we had with the living being we lost. Every tear, every memory, every moment of longing is a testament to the love that continues to live within us. I love this quote by Jamie Anderson: *"Grief is just love with no place to go"*.

My father passed away at the age of 53, approximately 40 years ago. There are still moments I am moved to tears when I think about him; I feel a longing to have one more day, even one more hour with him. I keep things that belonged to him, as a sweet memory. Of course these experiences changed over time and in general they became much less intense. Time does heal wounds, or soften our pain. I am sharing this example to underline that there is no rule for when grief should be over.

For this question, it is helpful to do some reading about the stages of grief. I refer to the Kübler-Ross Model, also known as the Five Stages of Grief, which offers a framework to understand the emotional responses following a significant loss. These stages are: Denial, Anger, Bargaining, Depression and Acceptance.

As coaches, we can offer a safe and caring space where our coachees can go through these stages. We can be there for them, with them. Hold the space with patience and respect.

We can invite them to explore their emotions rather than push them away or ignore them. We can ask their permission to take a closer look at the emotion they are not (fully) allowing to exist. Many of us 'toughen up' to avoid the world seeing our pain, our grief.

In the Co-Active Model we have the Principle of Process, where we ask for our coachee's permission to take a closer look at emotions they avoid. From both the coach and the coachee it often takes some or a lot of courage to slow down and explore these emotions. Normalising emotions as a natural part of being human can give the coachee the permission to examine what they have been trying to avoid.

As coaches we can acknowledge the coachee for who, and how, they are being to give themselves this permission. Without any rush, without the need to solve the 'problem'. An emotion is not a problem (!), it is a human experience and has a purpose. When we give ourselves the permission to be with our emotions, we will be more alive, even when we grieve the loss of a loved one.

***

Q55: How to support a coachee with challenging people in their environment?

There were several questions about how to coach someone who has someone in their life with whom it is really hard to be in a constructive and loving relationship. How to be with someone with narcissism, someone who is very controlling or manipulative?

The pitfall here is to start focusing on the 'problem'. How can we find a solution to be with such a person? First, that's not what coaching is about and, second, we coach the person experiencing the difficulty, not the 'difficult person'. We need to focus on what the coachee is experiencing, the impact on them of being in a relationship with such a person. Which of their values are being stepped on? Where might they have a 'stuck perspective' about this person? What is their emotional experience in this relationship and how are they being with these emotions? The Co-Active coach will recognise the three Principles of the Co-Active Model in these three questions.

Dear colleague, let's also take a closer look at other parts of the Co-Active Model. Rather than focusing on the issue, what else can you be curious about for this coachee? What are you actually hearing in their words, or in between the lines? What is your gut-feeling telling you? Or, which of your own thoughts, experiences or solutions might you need to self-manage? Where can you take the coachee into more exploration around this topic and what action wants to follow from there? Yes, these are the five Contexts in the Co-Active Model, the places I often describe as the 'come from' of the coach. A state of being.

Long story short, simply coach your coachee as you would on any other topic. It is not our job to find a solution for their problems, only to be thought-provoking and creative in how we help them look at a situation, or at another human being. From there on, it's their choice. They can choose how they want to be in that challenging relationship, and if they want to be in that relationship at all.

Their life, their choice.

***

Q56: What do you expect to be the future trends in coaching?

The profession of coaching has been evolving into a well-respected profession with high standards. Part of this, I believe, is due to the dedication of the key players in the world of coaching: the ICF and CTI. For decades, they've been working tirelessly to take coaching to the next level. Secondly, it is the commitment of the individual coaches who invested in a solid and ongoing education and made their accreditations a statement to the world: "I take this very seriously!".

The first trend I foresee is that it will become even more important that a coach gets certified and accredited, moving away from the idea that anyone can claim to be a coach. Okay, the title of coach is still, and probably will remain, an unprotected title. But not everyone can claim CPCC, or ACC/PCC/MCC behind their name.

Secondly, I expect a bigger connection between coaching and neuroscience. There is more and more research-based information showing coaching does transform something in people's brains, that people connect the dots in a new and permanent way.

Additionally, AI will find its way into coaching, as it has in many other professions. No, I don't believe AI will replace the coach, but coaches who refuse to use AI in one way or the other, will be replaced by those who do use it. This mirrors how things have evolved with other new technologies. For instance, when video-conferencing started, there were coaches who believed it was a danger for the profession. Nowadays the vast majority of coaches use it and we learned that it was a blessing for our profession.

I also see the professions of coaching and therapy growing closer and closer towards each other. This will not stop. I am convinced that we will get more and more therapists using coaching techniques, and that there will be more and more coaches investing in training and becoming licensed therapists.

Finally – without claiming this answer is complete – I believe coaches will create more partnerships and communities. Communities who will support and strengthen the individual. Partnerships so we can be more effective and efficient in how we do business. Coaches are likely to join larger organisations that handle sales and marketing for them. Alternatively, I envision small groups of coaches joining forces, and taking their collective resources and professional support to the next level. For instance, by forming a well-trained support team to manage scheduling, invoicing, websites, marketing and sales.

***

Q57: How to choose a Principle?

The following questions are from and for the Co-Active coaches amongst you, but also for people that are simply curious. Many questions came up about the three Principles in the Co-Active Model and these questions will be honoured by giving a summary of each Principle. For a more detailed description, I refer to the Co-Active Coaching book.

The Principles share the common purpose of being used in the exploration phase of the coaching session, helping the coachee to take a closer look at their topic and how they want to relate to it. What choices they want to make.

Sometimes our coachee is 'speaking in absolutes' when they introduce the topic they bring to the session. "It's always been like that, and it's never going to change. I tried everything, and nothing works". This is an indication they are 'stuck' in the way they look at the topic, they aren't able to see that situation or person in any other way than their current perspective. In this case we opt for Balance.

Or they would rather avoid experiencing the emotions they feel about something. It's too hard to have those feelings and they 'toughen up or shy away' from them. Here we opt for Process.

I could simplify by saying: "If it's not one of these two, go for Fulfillment". Additionally, there are times where the coachee gives clear hints that this Principle is the most relevant. For instance, when they need to choose between two options. Both are interesting, but they just wonder which of these two would be the best fit. Or they need to make another kind of choice towards their future. These are just two examples where it's clear that Fulfillment would serve the coachee best whilst exploring the topic at hand.

In the following three questions I will introduce the key elements of each Principle, without the intention to repeat what has already been explained in the Co-Active Coaching book.

***

Q57A: What are the essentials of the Co-Active Principle of Fulfillment?

From a meta perspective, the two key words in the Principle of Fulfillment are 'resonance' and 'dissonance'. In NPL (Normal People Language) one would say

“Life is good, I’m happy” versus “Bummer, this isn’t my best day”. This Principle is being used to explore what the coachee really wants, and what they (really) don’t want. Experiencing ‘dissonance’ is a normal part of life and it happens to all of us. If we don’t know what we don’t like, what is against our true and authentic self, it’s probably a lot harder to decide what it is we do want.

The Principle of Fulfillment comes with specific tools that can help the coachee gain more understanding of what’s right for them. And what isn’t. These tools are called Values, Life Purpose and Leader Within & Allies.

Values: our internal compass that guides us through life, enabling us to make choices aligned with our essence. Values are so personal and unique to the individual, that they’re sometimes compared to our DNA. While morals come from the world around us, values are very individual.

Life Purpose: some call it our Big Why and regardless of the name we give it, it’s a powerful tool to help the coachee find direction in their life. It is not a destination to reach, it’s more like a beacon on the horizon and as long as we travel in that direction, we know we’re on the right path. Co-Active coaches often work on a ‘Life Purpose Statement’ with their coachees, and this starts with a metaphor. That metaphor can capture the essence of the second part which reflects the impact one wants to have. Alternatively, the metaphor serves as an image of how this person would describe themselves. This tool is very powerful and it supports the coachee in making conscious decisions about the footprint they wish to leave while working towards their legacy.

Leader Within & Allies: this is an excellent example of how coaching and therapy can share tools, as this inspiring tool finds its origin in ‘Voice Dialogue’. Human beings are complex, multi-layered, and made up of multiple selves. This tool gives a voice to these ‘selves’ so they can be used as our personal advisors. The Leader Within is mostly seen as the wisest version of self where the Allies are seen as specialists in a specific situation. In Appendix 2 (Resources and Links) you will find a link to more info about Voice Dialogue if you’re curious to find out more.

These three tools are the main tools Fulfillment offers to explore resonance, but we can also do visioning work with the coachee. Exploring their dreams is also very helpful. In addition to these tools that create more connection to what resonates for the coachee, there are some tools that are designed to explore dissonance.

Saboteurs: the disturbing voices we start to hear when there's change in the air. I know there are many different theories about the Saboteur but I try to keep it very simple. The Saboteur is allergic to change and will play all kinds of tricks to maintain the status quo. Here's something interesting: coaching is all about change, so it can be seen as a compliment to the coaching process when the coachee's Saboteur becomes alarmed and starts playing its tricks. Simply put, all we need to do is explore what change is about to happen that woke up the Saboteur. Explore, for instance, which values are being honoured more with this change (or use the other resonance tools) and the Saboteur will be put to silence.

Limiting Beliefs: these can be described as old stories we keep telling ourselves but they're no longer serving us. Maybe they never did, maybe they did in a certain way but at this moment, they hold our coachee and their growth hostage. As long as the coachee is holding on to a belief that limits their growth, change is not even considered. A Limiting Belief will be 'defended' by our coachee trying to convince the coach that this is the way it should be. It takes courage from both the coach and the coachee to closely examine that old story and begin creating a new one – a belief that empowers them.

This concludes the brief introduction of this Principle. Again, if you want to take a deeper dive into this Principle, the Co-Active Coaching book is your resource.

***

Q57B: What are the essentials of the Co-Active Principle of Balance?

The key word of this super creative Principle for me is 'choice'. When we are stuck in the way we look at someone or something, we are not consciously choosing. Claiming back our choice is a way to claim back freedom.

When we work with this Principle, we start by making a clear distinction between the topic the coachee wants to explore and their current perspective on it. In general, they offer a mix of these two in a blur of words. As if they show us a plate of spaghetti bolognese and neither of us know where the beginning nor where the end is. Without this essential step, separating the topic and the current perspective, the coaching will be very, very difficult. After all these years I still love using this simple but very helpful phrase that can help us sort out this step: "It sounds like you're talking about_________ (the topic) and how you currently see this is _________(the current perspective)".

After looking into this current perspective a bit – no need to rub it in – you ask if the coachee is willing to explore other ways of looking at the same thing. This is where we start 'setting context'. It is as if you're going to play a new game so you need to look at the rules of that game. Otherwise, it'll be a mess. This is where the coach taps into the creativity of the coachee and their ability to freely associate. The coach might offer them a random object, ask what they see while looking out of the window, or inquire about which animal comes to mind. Really, anything goes! This is nothing but the starting point for them, to start creating a new perspective. As if they try on different pairs of glasses through which they look at their topic. Another metaphor is that they go shopping for new clothes and before making up their mind, they try on several outfits. Whilst exploring a few possible perspectives, the coach takes a moment each time to see what comes up for the coachee when they imagine becoming that perspective. To make the process easier, it's important to give each newly explored perspective a name, a label, and from there, look at the original topic. The coach simply asks what they see now, when they look at the topic through this other pair of glasses.

After exploring a few possible perspectives, the coach helps the coachee to quickly revisit them and choose one (or a combination) that speaks most to them at that moment. Using the wisdom of the Leader Within could be helpful when making this choice.

From there another fun part begins: brainstorming together! Without overthinking, try to come up with a good list of how one could show up in this newly chosen perspective and the things one could do. Coach and coachee both actively contribute to this list where quantity is more important than quality. The next step is when the coachee selects a few things from the big list they want to take to the next level. And before translating that into actionable steps, there's a beautiful little ritual, where the coachee commits to what they've chosen from the list. This is where 'Yes' becomes 'Hell Yes' and 'No' becomes 'Hell No'. That heartfelt commitment makes it feel as if the coachee signed a contract with themselves. And who wants to break a contract with themselves...?

Finally, the coachee decides which measurable action they choose to take after the coaching session. The coach will also discuss what kind of accountability would support the learning of the coachee in this matter.

It may feel like a rather rigid approach with so many steps. We could easily get lost in all of that. The fun thing is that the coach can also choose to only use specific elements of this Balance exercise instead of doing them all. To grow in confidence and competence as a coach, it's probably best to start with doing it 'by the book' before you decide to go freestyle.

***

Q57C: What are the essentials of the Co-Active Principle of Process?

This Principle feels like one of the things that sets Co-Active coaching aside from other coaching approaches. Rather than seeing emotions as a weakness, or as something that's only for therapists to work with, they're seen as a normal and healthy human experience. Human beings are emotional beings and it's been said that all our decisions are driven by emotions. When we play with the word 'emotion', we sometimes write it as 'e-motion'; energy in motion. Energy needs to be in motion. We need to experience our emotions to be fully alive. We need to feel the lows to fully get the highs. Many of us think we need to control and suppress our emotions. Emotions are perceived as a form of weakness. In Co-Active coaching, they're seen differently: emotions are a resource and are a place from which we can. They are an expression of aliveness. When our coachee is not allowing themselves to experience their emotions, they steal away parts of being alive, real and authentic. When an emotion is not (allowed to be) experienced, it's described as a 'stuck energy', a 'stuck emotion'.

In the Principle called Process, the intention is to invite the coachee to allow the emotions to be there, to process them and explore what becomes available when they give themselves that permission. Often the coachee is not even aware that they are suppressing a certain emotion. The coach is both the outsider and the one who knows their coachee very well, so there's a fair chance they will pick up on it when an emotion is suppressed. They feed that back to their coachee and when the recognition is mutual, the coach asks for permission to take a closer look at that emotion. Asking permission is an essential step! It is respectful to the coachee – who do we think we are to just assume it is okay for us to explore that emotion? – and it gives them the choice of whether they want to expand their emotional bandwidth. After they have given permission, the coach starts creating a 'metaphorical environment' to start exploring and to experience this emotion. Working with metaphors often makes it a lot easier for the coachee to look at the emotion. They can imagine the emotion is something outside of them and look at it, first from a distance and when they are ready, closer and closer. The coach offers a safe and, at the same time, courageous space, acknowledging and Championing the coachee. Often the pace is slow, the questions soft and short. Frequently, the coach only asks "What is here now?". Process is about consciously moving from one moment to the next, with deep respect and curiosity for what the coachee is experiencing in that very moment. It is not a strategic, step by step process, not as formulaic as the Balance Principle. It is a very conscious dance with the coachee. Sometimes slow, sometimes fast. There are no rules about the pace, nor about how much time one should spend processing the emotions. Sometimes just a few minutes are enough to 'set the stuck emotion free'. Sometimes it takes multiple sessions. As long as there is forward motion, it's fine. This often takes a lot of self-management from the coach. The coach might find it challenging to explore emotions themselves, or they start doubting their coaching skills when things take longer. Or they worry if the coachee 'will get anything out of it'. Well, when we see them as capable human beings who are able to find their way forward, we simply need to trust the process.

Some important coaching skills in this Principle are:

- Acknowledgement: sharing what you, at that moment, see in the essence of the coachee.
- Championing: what you believe is possible for them as you look toward the future.
- Articulate What is Going On: putting words on what you see, hear or sense and offer those to the coachee to explore.
- Name It: share with the coachee which emotion you sense they are not allowing to be present.
- Silence: dare to be silent, giving the coachee the space to experience what wants to be processed.
- Be With: holding the space for them, not shying away from whatever wants to happen and giving the coachee the feeling they are not alone.
- Powerful Questions: short, very open questions inviting the coachee to keep exploring.
- Inquiry: a Powerful Question 'on steroids' offered as homework, to consciously spend time with, maybe journal about.
- Metaphor: one image often says more than 1,000 words and can be very helpful to explore emotions.
- Embodiment: using the wisdom of the body to deepen the exploration of the emotion.
- Geography: the landscape created through the metaphor to make the experience even more real and rich.

The list is longer, of course, and two things need to be underlined: Active Listening and Self-Management. Process coaching requires an even deeper form of listening to everything the coachee is communicating. Their words, the intonation of these words, their gestures, and so on. Self-management is essential to avoid being overwhelmed by your own emotions as a coach, or being hijacked by your saboteurs. The coachee deserves your full and undivided presence.

The Principle of Process is as real as it is powerful and impactful. Many coaches have heard from their coachees that by doing this Process work, they found more emotional freedom and mental well-being than through years of therapy. I have tons of respect for the work of therapists, and coaches should not cross the line towards therapy (!), but I believe this Principle is impactful because the coach works with the coachee as someone who is not broken, who doesn't need to be fixed and whose potential they fully trust. Yes, this work takes courage from both the coach and the coachee, but when they give themselves the permission to go for it, they can move mountains.

***

Q58: Is there a coaching skill you would apply differently?

Actually, there is one! The last few years I have started to struggle with how we are teaching and applying the skill of accountability. As I often do, I went to the Merriam Webster dictionary to see what it teaches us about the meaning of this word. One of the things that came up is: "an obligation or willingness to accept responsibility or to account for one's actions". I see coaches who hold this lightly as well as coaches who take this rather literally. And if we don't provide clear context, there's a good chance our coachees will interpret this skill as being responsible for how they carried out the 'homework' or actions they committed to at the end of a coaching session.

Coaching is not about how well, or not, the coachee did the action and it is not homework like we got at school. The coach is not the teacher to whom the coachee should report about that 'homework'. The coach and the coachee partner up in a relationship which is based on being equals and with, at the end of the day, only one intention: the growth of the coachee. When the coach and the coachee reflect back on the action they decided to take in between the sessions, the question is always the same whether the coachee carried out the action, did it differently or not at all: "What can you learn from this?". But looking at how 'accountability' is often used in coaching, it feels like we could do with an update.

The term 'accountability' is often confused with another coaching skill, described as 'structure'. In this context a 'structure' is nothing but a simple reminder to help the coachee remember the action. This could be a reminder in their agenda, a picture on their phone, a sticky note on their desk or the mirror, or whatever the coach and the coachee can think of. In essence, anything goes. I think this reminder can be very supportive for our coachee because in their busy life, it is easy to forget things. This is something we can likely all relate to.

So 'accountability' is not a reminder and it is not about taking responsibility, it is all about the learning. As shown in the 'Awareness Cycle' in Appendix 1, coaching is about creating awareness for the coachee. In my view, 'accountability' is simply another way to achieve new awareness through the learning gained from their actions. This is why I would vote for another way to set up the last part of a coaching session. I'd primarily like to use different words to describe the different steps. After telling the coachee that the session is about to come to an end, we can ask them what they have learned so far about the topic they have explored. The next thing is to ask them what kind of action they want to take from there, or the coach suggests an action. After designing this with the coachee, the coach might ask what would help them remember to follow through on the action – the 'structure'. Finally, the coach can invite the coachee to reflect on how they want to capture the learning from the action. Maybe the word for reflecting on an action could simply be 'reflection'? Maybe that's the new word for 'accountability'?

Q59: What about coaching and Diversity & Inclusion?

I've reserved this question for near the end of this book.

The reason is that to address this question, I felt like sharing the chapter from my book *Golden Rules for Coaching* where I've shared my vision on this. So, here it is, the 15th 'Golden Rule':

'This Golden Rule is more than an attempt to say something politically correct. It's something that was a belief in coaching well before the world started to take a serious stand for huge groups of the world population who weren't treated with the respect they deserve.

It moves me to tears when I see people being mistreated for their race, gender, faith, sexuality, social or cultural background or whatever reason one has to hold themselves as superior over another human being.

In coaching land, we don't often use the word 'wrong' yet here I do use it. It is WRONG to judge people for who they are, for their background or for any other reason used to justify treating them as less worthy or making them feel that way.

It's ethically and morally just not right, aka wrong...

Whilst some people have the talent to take a stand through political processes or the like, I'd better not. I'm way too direct and will probably lose my patience quickly. It's really important and necessary work and I'm grateful for those who use their talents for these purposes. It's more than just work, it's a mission!

Through my work as a coach I'm also on a mission: 'to positively influence the lives of 10 million people'. I've chosen to work towards this goal by touching one life after the other. By trusting the ripple effect of the work with all those individuals. By training and mentoring other coaches so they can join the 'Army of Positive Change'.

I've never met a single coach who judged their coachees for one of the reasons mentioned above. Inspired by their high personal moral standards, the Code of Ethics and their vision of humanity they choose to see a human being above and beyond whatever category the world labels them with. Coaches work with prisoners and presidents. Okay, they might not like what the prisoner (or the president) has done, they might hate the 'sin', yet love the 'sinner'.

The coach chooses to see the light in somebody, their spirit, the divine in the human being.

Not the colour of their eyes, not the skin on the outside. Not their age, not their race. No, they look at their light.

Not the mistakes they've made, not the dreams they let go of. I'm quoting from a beautiful song 'I Am Light' by India.Arie which is something I frequently ask my coachees to listen to.

Because there is something weird happening. Many of us do not dare to see our own light. We keep ourselves small, make ourselves wrong. We developed an image about ourselves that's based on Limiting Beliefs and 'Negativations'. Borrowed from my book Awareness Builder 101: 'Many of us call ourselves names, say things about ourselves that are utterly mean and harmful. Hurting our own hearts with our own words, with a tongue as sharp as a double-edged sword. Cutting right through our soul'. These kind of words I call Negativations.

In coaching it's not so much about taking a stand for a category of people who're being mistreated, who're not granted the respect for who they are and how they want to live their life. In coaching we take a stand for the individual who we're working with.

Frequently this means pointing them at the Negativations they speak about themselves. The stories they think that are true, or should be true, yet in reality are a lie. A lie about whom they are at their core. Stories made up by themselves or told to them by others. Stories that make them see (so called) limitations instead of all of their creativity and resources. These resources are wildly diverse and multi-faceted. This diversity is to be encouraged and further awakened. It's gold living inside of the coachee and it wants to come to the surface.

The coach calls it out when the coachee is not empowering themselves. The coach is looking for the gold and the diamonds in the coachee. What may seem like a simple rock, may hold that diamond. So we don't ignore anything from the coachee, we include 'the good, the bad and the ugly'. All is allowed to be and to be created from. Sometimes this means we need to work through the mud, walk through a desert, climb a mountain, cross an ocean.

Yet with courage and including the brilliance that lives inside of every human being, thus also the coachee we're working with, going through the mud may bring gold to the surface, the sand in the desert will become glass and crystals, mountains can be moved and we can surf the waves of the ocean.

For such a mind-blowing process we need to see, acknowledge, include and create from all of the diversity of the coachee. In order to live up to their birthright.

Stealing somebody's birthright away from them is wrong. Supporting somebody to bring their birthright to life is a blessing and a privilege to witness'.

***

Q60: What was the most beautiful day of your life?

I remember the exact moment I got this question. It was during the Q&A party we hosted to celebrate my 60th birthday, when we started collecting the questions for this book. It moved me to tears and I immediately felt the answer. It's not a secret but it is the most personal thing I share in this book.

I can think of many beautiful moments in life, like various amazing things I experienced together with my wife, during my travels or the moments where my life was saved when I was close to knocking on heaven's door. Yet my heart fills with a deep gratitude and tons of pride when I think back to the day when I climbed a mountain with my son. He struggled with addictions for a long, long time. It was hard for him to get to the top of that mountain because, and it's putting it mildly, he was not in the best mental and physical condition. His body close to being ruined by alcohol and drugs, his spirit numbed.

For years I tried to convince him to give up his addictions. Sometimes kindly, often not so. Driven by my own fears and so called 'brilliant ideas' about how to solve this problem. I was convinced I knew best. But I totally missed the point. I coached many, many people where I fully trusted them and was fully convinced they were the specialists of their life. That they could change their path by making different choices. But with my own son, I couldn't. I tried everything, except fully trusting him.

That day something shifted. There was no blame, nor advice.

On top of that mountain, I saw him looking into the far distance, impressed by the 360 view. It was as if he could see into the future. Future: something he hadn't been able to see for so long.

We talked. We laughed. We cried. We were together. Though not his coach (!), I could finally self-manage my solutions and instead, 'just' be with him. Be curious. Allowing him to process thoughts and feelings in his own way, allowing him to connect the dots.

It was a beautiful day because I got clean from being a problem solver. It was a beautiful day because he decided to go to rehab and look the monsters of his addictions in the eyes. He has been clean and sober ever since. He is stronger than I am because I sometimes fall back into the old habit of trying to fix other's problems.

It was the most beautiful day in my life because I got my son back. It was the most beautiful day in my life because he claimed his life back.

Though I am not responsible for the choices he made leading to addiction, I am responsible for how I held him in all of this.

And it was only when I understood and accepted that I couldn't save him, that he has the right to make his own choices and that he is responsible for the consequences of his choices, that I could see him for the man he actually is. Not the addict, but the man. The man I love so dearly because he is my son, which made it so unbelievably hard for me not to try and 'rescue' him. He could have jumped from the mountain that day, but instead he jumped into life. Through his own self-empowered choice.

Here I am, with tears in my eyes again whilst writing this. But the old tears have been washed away and replaced with tears of joy, gratitude and pride.

I sometimes still find it challenging not to 'go for the rescue' with the people close to me. As a coach, I can generally self-manage that. As a partner, as a father, as a friend, as a son and in other private roles one has, I sometimes 'fall off the wagon'. When they ask for help, or when I ask if they need some help, that's different. Yet all my unsolicited advice, in essence holds the message that I don't fully trust them.

So sometimes I climb a mountain, or find another place in nature, where I take a moment to reflect on how I could love these people even more by seeing them as deeply creative and resourceful, without me having to fix them.

Yes, back to this cornerstone in the Co-Active Model that tells us that People are Naturally, Creative, Resourceful and Whole. This part of the model jumps out for me, together with the Context of Curiosity, because they hold so many lessons for me. I am so grateful for these lessons and I bow deeply to Karen and Henry Kimsey-House, Phillip Sandahl and Laura Whitworth for co-writing the Co-Active book and sharing their knowledge with us. What they have created has impacted countless lives, including mine, and made the world a better place.

I am convinced that, on the beautiful day up there on that mountain, the ripple effect of the Co-Active Model saved my son's life and it made mine so much richer.

Epilogue

It was an intense but joyful process to write this book. The words just flowed out of me and I hope they will inspire you. This book is a celebration and an expression of my purpose:

I am an awareness builder who inspires and supports the Army of Positive Change

I am grateful for the questions you gave me from which I could create. Each question I receive also holds a lesson for me. So thank you!

My longing for you is that you will find lessons in this book that you can apply in your coaching as well as in your personal life.

I am not claiming that the answers provided in the book are the only possible answers. There are more answers, for sure also better answers. As an 'Imperfectionizt' I never strive to find the perfect answer. In fact, if I were to revisit some of these questions a year from now, my responses might change. I will keep questioning my own answers and I encourage you to do the same. Because I believe that if we all seek constant improvement, our 'Army of Positive Change' will grow stronger and make a greater impact together.

Thank you for reading this book.

Be Well & Do Good,

Appendix 1: The Awareness Cycle

Coaching is primarily about creating new and more Awareness for the coachee about who they are in their essence and how they want to show up in life.

Awareness comes with a responsibility: making clear Choices in line with that Awareness.

Choices without specific Action are just interesting thoughts.

The coach calls the coachee forth to take specific Action in between the coaching sessions.

The coach designs with the coachee what kind of Accountability would support the coachee with this Action and to create learning from how the Action was taken (or not taken).

This learning leads to new Awareness and with that the Cycle continues and becomes an ongoing process of growth and transformation.

Appendix 2: Resources and Links

The Kindle version of this book, holds many links to a wide variety of resources.

To get access to these links, please go to a special page on the author's website: www.alexverlek.nl/links

Here you will find more info about:

- More info about the author and his coaching services
- Alex's Group Supervision & mentoring program for CPCCs
- The programs of the Co-Active Training Institute (CTI)
- Where to order the Co-Active Coaching book
- The Co-Active Coaching Certification programme
- A webinar about this Certification programme
- The Co-Active Leadership programme
- The Co-Active Leadership Workshop (CLW)

CO-ACTIVE®
TRAINING INSTITUTE

- The International Coaching Federation (ICF)
- The ICF Code of Ethics
- The Association for Coaching
- The ORSC-training for Team Coaching
- The Get Clients Now! By programme by CJ Hayden
- 'The Prosperous Coach' by Steve Chandler & Rich Litvin
- The Imposter Syndrome
- The website from Drs. Stone about Voice Dialogue

Appendix 3: Structure Your Session Cheat Sheet

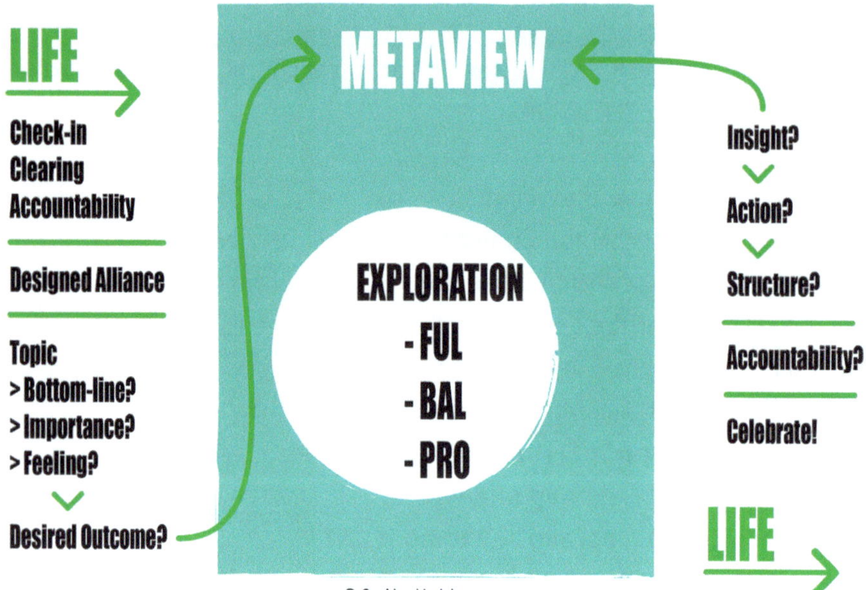

© By Alex Verlek

You want your own copy of this cheat sheet?
Just download a free copy from my website:
https://alexverlek.nl/108010/

Appendix 4: YOU

(Poem written for the Co-Active Fulfillment workshop)

You
meant to be
You

Designed to become
the star that lives in you
the magic that wants to break free

You're born to claim
your reason to be
the dreams that want to be lived

Trust the truth that lives in you
so you dare to have the impact
which creates the footprint
leading towards your legacy
Yours, no one else's.
Yours!

Because you
are meant to be You
Waiting for the right moment?
If not now, then when?!

Because you
are meant to be you
with every breath
with every step
and every life you touch

Yet, sometimes, you will be scared
questioned and challenged
even by yourself
Voices of doubt will whisper in your ear

Be aware!
This is not the truth
which is told by your most empowered self
That's the voice that knows
You

Because you
are meant to be
You

Be aware!
You
are not alone
You're part of an army
An army of positive change
Fighting a different battle
with different weapons
like love and a longing to grow
potential, purpose and dreams
waiting in the other You

Like a candle
you light another candle
you multiply by sharing
Calling forth light
in the other You

Because you
are light
meant to be spread

I am light

Printed in Poland
by Amazon Fulfillment
Poland Sp. z o.o., Wrocław

50245755R10095